漢語交流

初級漢語閱讀書寫本

Cynthia Ning

夏威夷大學

耶魯大學遠東出版社

COMMUNICATING IN CHINESE

READING AND WRITING

Communicating in Chinese: an interactive approach to beginning Chinese
Student's Book for Reading and Writing

Library of Congress Cataloging in Publications data:

Ning, Cynthia
    Communicating in Chinese: Student's Book for Reading and Writing
        includes index
        ISBN 978-0-887-10178-6
        1. Chinese language-Textbooks for foreign speakers-English
        2. College readers. I. Title
            1994

Managing Editor: John S. Montanaro
Cover designer: Nancy Jo Fumaro

13 12 11 10

......................CONTENTS

Acknowledgements

People who gave freely of their talents, resources, and energy have buoyed me since the inception of this project.

Stephen Fleming (University of Hawaii) let me pillage his notes from a first-year Chinese class he taught using *Communicating in Chinese*. These included several very nice reading activities that he developed, which I have incorporated here. I offered to make him a co-author if he would collaborate with me more extensively, but although he was willing, he was too busy completing a second Master's degree (in ESL) and teaching full-time to follow through. Still, his support and keen editorial eye have been most valuable.

Cornelius Kubler (Williams College) sent me the negatives of his entire collection of photographs of Chinese signs. Many of these photographs appear in this volume. I was breath-taken when I saw the photographs, and continue to be impressed by Neil's generosity.

Another friend who lent her support is Karen Steffen Chung (National Taiwan University). Visiting her lovely home outside Taipei, I startled my hosts by rooting through wastebaskets in search of "authentic reading material." Karen subsequently sent me two boxes of the debris of daily living in Taiwan. Several items from these have been included here.

Lasting inspiration and some prime authentic texts were also provided by Richard Chi (University of Utah) and Ted Yao (Mt. Holyoke College), with whom I'm very happy to have been able to work on several projects over the years. David Hiple, associate director of the National Foreign Language Resource Center and director of the Second Language Teaching and Curriculum Center at the University of Hawaii, provided guidance in reading methodology, and accompanied me on some long treks in Hong Kong to gather (and photograph) more samples of reading texts.

A number of photographs by Allan Awaya and William Crampton that appeared in *Book I* are repeated here, as are some drawings from *The Chinese Word Book* (Bess Press). Some shots of streets signs by William Crampton are included as well.

I thank the many people whose special language and technical skills have been invaluable to this project. Ping Hao, Yuqing Bai, Hai-yen Huang, Chenshan Tian, Xiaolin Wang, and Lei Ye, all of Hawaii's Center for Chinese Studies, wrote most of the notes that illustrate handwriting and informal written style. They were a ready and able source of consultation on many points of language usage, and of documents as necessary (Ping Hao's graduation certificate appears here). Chin-tang Lo of the Department of East Asian Languages and Literatures agreed to allow a note he left on my desk to be published. Daniel Cole, editor of *China Review International* and coordinator of the Center for Chinese Studies, obtained all the computer hardware and software I used to piece together camera-ready copy of the manuscript. He consulted with me on technique and layout, fielded phone calls and handled business when I needed to focus on the manuscript, and tolerated many incursions into his personal space because his was the best computer. Samples of his fine hand in Chinese appear here as well.

Student assistant Ip Hung Mar scanned, pixel-edited, photocopied and collated.

My daughter Robyn Yee wrote an autobiographical note and drew a self-portrait to serve as her "passport photograph" for the unit on the family.

The calligrapher featured on the cover of this volume is Professor Fan Zhang of the Henan Teacher's University, an acclaimed poet, painter, and calligrapher. He is perhaps best known for being able to create calligraphic scrolls by writing with both hands at the same time.

Drafts of the manuscript were edited and proofread by a number of individuals associated with the Center: Dong Liu, instructor of Chinese at Beijing's Qinghua University; Hai-yen Huang, instructor of Chinese at the Inter-University Program and the Mandarin Training Center in Taipei; Chenshan Tian, former editor at *New World Press*; Yuqing Bai, formerly a journalist with *People's Daily;* and Stephen Fleming, instructor of Chinese. Chenshan Tian developed the first draft and proofread the final draft of the indices that appear at the end of the book. John Montanaro of Far Eastern Publications provided several pages of editorial notations and some very helpful suggestions for improvement. Final scrutiny of the entire manuscript was provided by my parents Grace and Chung-fong Ning.

I thank the University of Hawaii's Center for Chinese Studies and National Foreign Language Resource Center for their constant monetary, staff and collegial support, and for having created an environment that encourages experimentation with language teaching methodologies.

Finally, I am grateful to my husband Allan and daughter Robyn Yee for their patience and support, and to my parents for making dinner nearly every night.

Introduction (for the Student)

Communicating in Chinese, Listening and Speaking, focused on speaking Chinese. *Reading and Writing* will teach you, first, to understand pieces of simple written Chinese texts—signs, schedules, advertisements, hand-written notes, as well as transcriptions of simulated spoken discourse. It is important to remember that you **need not try to puzzle out every word of every text.** (You don't read every word of every text in your native language. When you receive a postcard, for example, chances are you read the interesting, relevant part—the message—and ignore the rest—the cancellation, where the postcard was printed, etc.) Instructions accompanying each text in this book will direct you to pieces of it that are appropriate or useful to you. While you are encouraged to skim through the remainder to see what you make of it, please focus on what you **can** understand and don't be discouraged by what you can't. When you arrive in a Chinese community and are faced with a pandemonium of character texts, you will need to be able to screen out what you can't understand and focus in on what you can, and try to extract a meaning, a message, from what you can decipher. Do begin developing this skill now, as you proceed through this book.

The second thing this reading and writing text will teach you is how to convey simple messages by writing Chinese. There are at least two parts to this process: one is to learn how to form basic characters and another is how to string them together in meaningful sequences, to express what you want to say. Whereas over 1,000 characters are introduced to you in various combinations and contexts **for reading recognition only**, this book will only teach you to **hand-write** some 300 characters. Using these basic characters, you will be able to fill in your personal information (name, address, telephone, age, gender, etc.) on forms, write simple notes to make or rearrange appointments, write brief statements concerning personal preferences in food, clothing, etc., and otherwise express your own meaning in simple interactions with Chinese people. You will also gain a rudimentary understanding of the characteristics of the Chinese script.

Following are further points to keep in mind.
•Beginning in the mid-1950s, the government of the People's Republic of China began to promulgate simplified versions of Chinese characters (説=说, 寫=写) in an effort to boost China's literacy rate. These **simplified** characters are currently in use in the PRC and Singapore, while Taiwan (the Republic of China), Hong Kong, and many overseas Chinese communities continue to use **traditional** characters. Given the level of interchange among all these Chinese locales, however, plus the fact that foreigners in contact with the Chinese will sooner or later have contact with both sides, this textbook teaches both forms for reading recognition. We therefore expect that you will learn to read both simplified and traditional character texts. For writing, however, we suggest that you pick either one form or the other (both are taught) and learn to write that form exclusively. Some students pick the simplified form for expediency, or because they expect to spend time in the PRC. Others pick traditional characters for their form and beauty, because they wish to communicate with relatives who write traditional characters, etc. Whichever you decide upon, try not to mix them up, at least not within the same note/letter/document!
•A "Prelude" and three "Interludes" in this book will focus your attention on components of Chinese characters. **Radicals** are meaning components—they generally succeed in giving you a hint of the meaning of the character, such as "of the plant kingdom," "relating to thought and emotion," and "relating to speech." There are a total of some 200 radicals in Chinese, of which some 50 are commonly used. For each character introduced for writing in this book, the radical is identified for your convenience. These are useful to learn to recognize for the future, when you may want to begin using Chinese diction-

6

aries. Similarly, a **phonetic** is a sound component, which will sometimes succeed in giving you a hint of how a character is pronounced. If you want to learn more about radicals, look in Chinese-English dictionaries such as *Mathew's Chinese English Dictionary. The Five Thousand Dictionary: Chinese-English* by Courtenay Hughes Fenn identifies both the radicals and the phonetics of 5,000 common Chinese characters, but is now out of print (you can try to locate a copy in a library).

•Stroke order (the order in which you write each stroke in a character) is indicated for writing characters by a number placed near the start point of each stroke. (However, it is expected that you will need writing help from a teacher as well.) **Do memorize stroke order**; it will help you read and write cursive script or use a dictionary in the future. Some simple hints about stroke order:

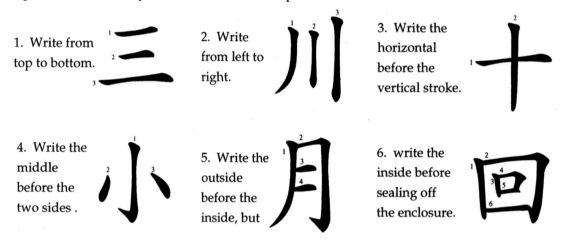

1. Write from top to bottom.

2. Write from left to right.

3. Write the horizontal before the vertical stroke.

4. Write the middle before the two sides .

5. Write the outside before the inside, but

6. write the inside before sealing off the enclosure.

•Finally, a note about Chinese punctuation. You'll notice two types of commas in the renditions of discourse in this book: one is the usual comma separating two thoughts (，) and the other is the "enumerative comma" used when listing items (、) . The following English passage illustrates (approximately) the use of both kinds, as well as of the Chinese period (。) .

I've been away ， so I hope you'll forgive this late response 。 I'd like to order green 、 white 、 blue 、 and black banners for the reception ， and to have them placed at the front entrance 、 over the podium 、 by the side entrance 、 and along the entire back wall 。 Thank you 。

Remember, learning a new language takes you into a new culture. It brings you into contact with a new people. You can't hope to learn everything overnight (or even in a lifetime)! Be patient, be constant, enjoy what you are learning, ask lots of questions, go back over old lessons to see if you can pick up new insights, look ahead into new lessons to get a feel for what's coming, talk to your classmates to see if your understanding of the material is the same as theirs, seek out native speakers when you can to try out your skills, pick up a Chinese publication and skim through it for words, phrases, maybe even a sentence? you can decipher, play "what's this character" games with friends who know some Chinese, pass notes in Chinese in class, and keep in mind that you are communicating in the language of at least one-fifth of the world's population.

Introduction (for the Teacher)

Communicating in Chinese, Reading and Writing presents the reading and writing curriculum for an introductory course in standard Chinese. The vocabulary of written Chinese is in many cases different from spoken (yí kuài qián vs. yì yuán). Furthermore, what the student might need to say and decipher in speech in a given context is often not what s/he needs to read or to write in that same context. In shopping, for example, the student might require facility in the following:

Q: "Zhèi ge duóshǎo qián?"   A: "Wǔ kuài liù máo qián."

However, s/he might benefit more from being able to comprehend texts such as 特價：五元 or 售票處 than from a written transcription of the spoken discourse. Thus, the listening/speaking and the reading/writing curricula are linked in terms of **context** (setting, topic) and **function** (what the students do in the given context), but might very well differ in terms of specific **content** (vocabulary items, sentence patterns), although a great deal of overlap exists as well.

The performance goals of this curriculum are keyed to the proficiency levels promulgated by the American Council on the Teaching of Foreign Languages (ACTFL). Simplified proficiency level descriptions for reading and writing, based on ACTFL's generic and Chinese-specific descriptions, are as follows.

Reading

Novice Level Able to recognize isolated words and/or major phrases when supported by context.

Intermediate Level Able to read for instructional and informational purposes standardized messages, phrases or expressions from simple connected texts dealing with basic personal and social needs.

Advanced Level Able to comprehend main ideas and facts of connected descriptive or narrative prose, such as news items, short stories, personal correspondence and simple technical material written for the general reader.

Superior Level Able to read with nearly complete comprehension expository prose in a wide variety of texts, including those which treat unfamiliar topics and situations.

Writing

Novice Level Able to reproduce from memory some familiar words and phrases in character form, as well as recombinations of these.

Intermediate Level Able to meet a limited number of practical writing needs, such as supplying key personal information on simple forms and documents and writing short messages about personal preferences, daily routine, everyday events, and other topics grounded in personal experience.

Advanced Level Able to write routine social correspondence, cohesive summaries and resumes, as well as narratives and descriptions of a factual nature.

Superior Level Able to write most types of correspondence, such as memos as well as social and business letters, and short research papers and statements of position in areas of special interest or in special fields.

This curriculum aims to bring students to the **Intermediate** level in reading and writing. In reading, it seeks to develop the students' ability to puzzle out pieces of selected authentic texts relating to survival needs, and to identify key facts and some details in carefully written personal communication. In addition, students are led to puzzle through transcriptions of simple, simulated oral discourse based on the listening-speaking curriculum. For writing, it focuses on developing the student's ability to provide biodata on simple forms and write a variety of brief messages relating to daily, survival issues.

To achieve these ends, the curriculum utilizes a range of materials from a variety of sources. Forms, photographs of signs, menus, printed and handwritten notes, teacher-created simulated texts form the bulk of the volume. Some key characteristics resulting from the ways in which these texts are incorporated and developed into an identifiable curriculum are the following.

8

•The texts are representative of real language used in a variety of Chinese communities in the PRC, Taiwan, Hong Kong, and the US. The content of some of these texts may strike some native-speaking Chinese as unorthodox or substandard—not worthy of appearing in a textbook. Since the materials are eclectic, they may also disturb some native speakers because they are to an extent "foreign" (from a different Chinese community) and therefore unfamiliar. And finally, materials that were selected because of their link to American culture (McDonald's ads) and presumed therefore to appeal to the American learner may be panned by native Chinese for being "un-Chinese."

Some egregious examples exhibiting the "flaws" listed above have been discarded. What remains are materials that I hope can be tolerated (if grudgingly) by most native speakers. They represent real rather than idealized language, and are therefore fair to present to students.

•Since the reading-writing curriculum (like the listening-speaking curriculum) is task-based, not all of every text needs to be decoded. Instructions direct the student's attention towards that portion of the text that is either necessary to accomplish a task ("find out how much X costs"), or that teaches vocabulary that is useful and learnable at this point. The remainder of the text can (and should) simply be ignored. It is hoped that at least those bits of language receiving focus in each text (if not the whole text) are acceptable to all native speakers of Chinese.

•No matter whether students intend to deal with Hong Kong-Taiwan Chinese or with PRC-Singapore Chinese in the future, there is so much interchange among Chinese communities these days that they will need to be able to read both simplified and traditional forms of Chinese characters. This curriculum proceeds under the assumption, then, that students will learn both forms. Indeed, if both forms are taught simultaneously (for reading recognition only), the process is perhaps easier than if the students were to grow accustomed to one form alone, and then had to learn the other form under duress. For writing, it is assumed that students will be allowed to choose to write either one form or the other, preferably exclusively—at least they should not switch back and forth between simplified and traditional styles within the same document! Native Chinese generally write either one form or the other. Since most can read both forms (protestations notwithstanding), this does not generally constitute a problem.

•Transcriptions of simulated oral discourse are included to provide students exposure to texts of longer length than the excerpts of authentic documents that are suitable to their level. These transcriptions are therefore inauthentic by their very nature. This "inauthenticity" may be exacerbated by the fact that they were composed with the non-native learner in mind: to an extent the cultural norms of the target culture have purposely been compromised to accomodate the cultural realities of the learner's native (presumed American/Western) culture. The dialogues are lively rather than staid (and safe) to give the learner an incentive to keep puzzling through unfamiliar characters. Although native speakers of Chinese have complained that these are not entirely representative of their speech styles (too direct, sometimes linguistically oversimplified), I hope that such infelicities can be tolerated in the interest of holding the student's attention.

This volume is highly experimental, and therefore susceptible to some controversy. Fortunately, in this age of computers, corrections are painless. Perhaps future editions can rectify shortcomings found in this one. Your feedback is therefore welcome and solicited.

Draw lines matching the Chinese numbers to the Arabic numerals.
(Guess if you don't know!)

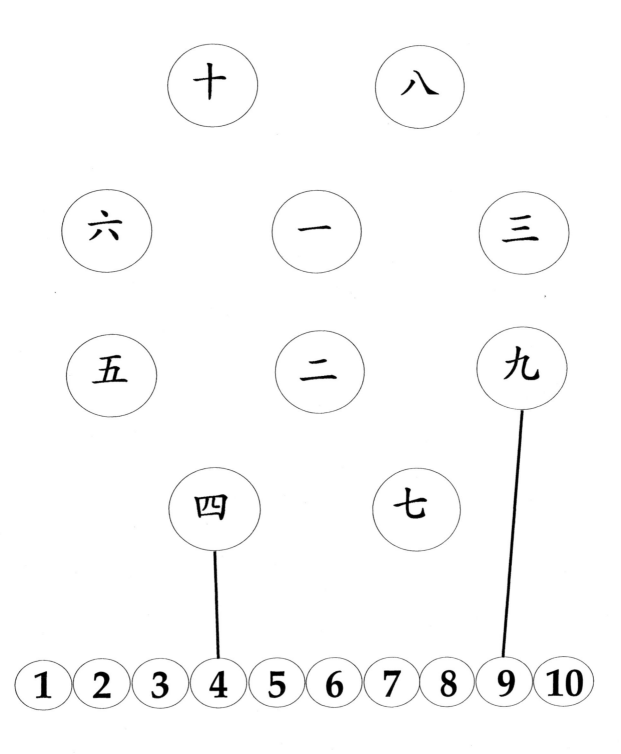

Write the numbers, following the stroke order indicated.

character	radical 一 *pinyin* yī English *one*
一	

	二 èr *two*
二	

	一 sān *three*
三	

	口 sì *four*
四	

	二 wǔ *five*
五	

	八 liù *six*
六	

	一 qī *seven*
七	

	八 bā *eight*
八	

	乙 jiǔ *nine*
九	

	十 shí *ten*
十	

1. The earliest records of Chinese characters on oracle bone inscriptions included versions that were more pictographic than Chinese characters today. Match these "pictographic" characters on the right with their English equivalents on the left.

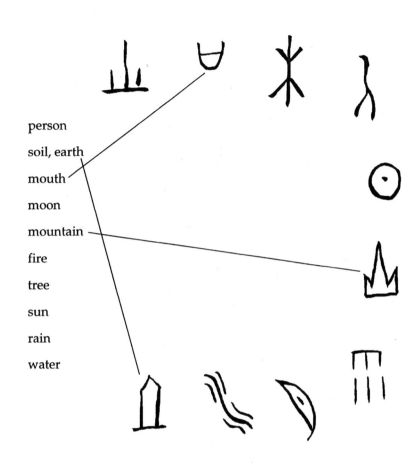

person

soil, earth

mouth

moon

mountain

fire

tree

sun

rain

water

火　　口　　木　　人　　日　　山

2. Now, based on what you know about the pictographs, can you figure out what these modern characters mean?

土　　水　　月　　雨

3. Label each character in item 2 above with one of the following identifications.

rén (human, person)	tǔ (soil, earth)	shuǐ (water)	yǔ (rain)	mù (tree, wood)
shān (mountain)	kǒu (mouth)	rì (sun)	huǒ (fire)	yuè (moon)

4. Each of the ten characters on the previous page is a *radical* or "meaning component" of a Chinese character. Circle the radicals you recognize in the following characters.

嶺 mountain range	旦 dawn, day	雲 clouds	吹 to blow
峰 peak, summit	映 shine, reflect	雪 snow	吞 to swallow
峽 canyon, gorge	晚 evening, night	雷 thunder	喝 to drink
朔 new moon	地 earth, land	址 site, location	林 forest
朧 rising moon	墳 grave, tomb	枯 withered	松 pine tree

5. Some radicals can be somewhat altered when they combine with another character component. Match the full forms on the left below with the combination form on the right.

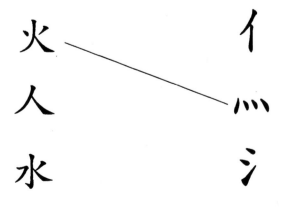

火　　　　　亻

人　　　　　灬

水　　　　　氵

6. Circle the radicals in the following characters.

燈　　　　焦　　　　熱　　　　仙

lantern, light　　　to scorch　　　hot　　　an immortal

濺　　　　波　　　　傭　　　　你

to splash, splatter　　wave, ripple　　a servant　　you

7. Try to pick out the radicals in the characters below.

楚　　司　　坤　　晶　　位

侶　　崩　　岳　　有　　森

唱　　棟　　洋　　炒　　暗

海　　塊　　吃　　露　　煙

基　　僑　　需　　崎　　期

梧　　溪　　朗　　煮　　只

8. Write the radicals, following the stroke order indicated.

Basic courtesy expressions

请···

謝謝 。

不謝 。

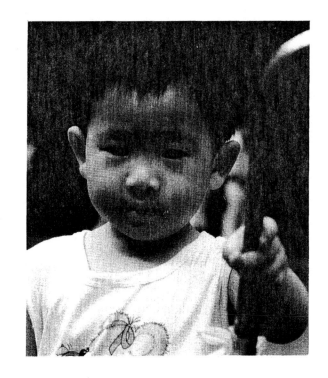

你 好 !

再 見 。

1. Read aloud with a partner.

   Two friends bump into each other coming out of the subway.

   A.　你 好 。　Hello.

   B.　你 好 。　Hello.

   A.　請 ···　Go ahead...

   B.　謝謝 。　Thank you.

   A.　不謝 。　You're welcome.

   B.　再見 。　Goodbye.

   A.　再見 。　Goodbye.

2. Match the complex characters on the left with the simplified characters on the right.

   請

   謝謝

   再見

   谢谢

   再见

   请

3.   "Please don't park by the window. Thank you."

- Circle and label "thank you."

- Circle and label "please."

- Circle and label "don't." (Actually, the sign says, "Window. Please don't park. Thank you.")

4.   "Please don't smoke"

- Fill in the blank.

    _____ wù xī yān.

- Guess which character means "to breathe in, to inhale." Circle and label it.
- Guess which character indicates the noun "smoke." Circle and label it.
- What does 勿 mean? Write the English equivalent.

_____

(This word is in literary style—it is generally used in writing rather than speech.)

5. On the following page are the opening and closing lines of a letter written by a 12-year old to her mother.

•Circle the words "Hello!" and "goodbye." (Notice the use of the polite form 您 in place of the informal 你.)

•The author of the letter opens with the salutation "Dear Mom." Circle this.

•She closes with "Your daughter Miaomiao," followed by the date. Circle this.

•Check one. This letter is written in ☐ traditional
                                  ☐ simplified characters.

亲爱的妈妈：

　　您好！许多日子没给您写信了，请您原谅。快到新年了，我特意寄几个贺年片给您，那个友谊袋是我做的，好看吗？人家都说我做得挺好的，我想您也会很喜欢的。"每逢佳节倍思亲"，是啊，我们一家人分地三洲，不能相见，只能用信来表达自己的思念之情。

．
．

　　好了，今天就谈到这吧，别忘了替我向爸爸问好，再见！
　　祝

节日愉快　　身体健康　　工作顺利

女儿苗苗

1986.12.28.

6. Summary. For each word in English, fill in the *pinyin*, the corresponding number for traditional characters (T) and the corresponding letter for simplified characters (S).

English	*pinyin*	T	S
Hello.			
Please.., go ahead.			
Thank you.			
You're welcome.			
Goodbye.			
Don't... (literary)	wù		
to smoke			
you (formal)			

1. 不謝　　a. 您

2. 吸煙　　b. 你好

3. 你好　　c. 谢谢

4. 勿　　　d. 请

5. 謝謝　　e. 再见

6. 請　　　f. 不谢

7. 再見　　g. 吸烟

8. 您　　　h. 勿

7. Learn to write the characters below. The numbers indicate stroke order; each number is written near the beginning point of the stroke it marks.

8. Pretend you are writing your parents a Chinese letter. Write the opening and closing salutations in the blanks. ➡

9. Pretend you are making a sign for your room. Fill in the blanks below in characters.

"No Smoking, Please. Thank You."

── 勿吸煙 。____ ____

親愛的爸爸、媽媽：

_____ ____ ！ x x

x x x x x x x x x x x x x x x x x x x x x x x

x x x x x x x x x x x x x x x x x x x x x x x

_____ _____ ！

兒 _____
　　(write your name)

SEGMENT A: Own name, personal names.

1. This is part of a PRC alien registration form, to be completed upon check-in at a hotel. Fill in the *pinyin* in the empty bubbles.

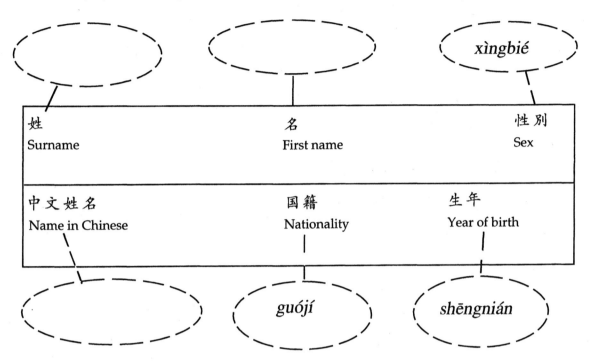

2. Read aloud with a partner.

Chen and Ma are chatting at a Western-style cocktail party.

馬：她姓甚麼？   What is her last name?

陳：姓李。   It's Li.

Later, Li and Chen talk at the party.

李：他叫甚麼名字？   What is his first name?

陳：誰？   Whose?

李：他。   His.

陳：他叫…   His name is...

Ma comes up with another acquaintance.

你們好！   Hello!

3. Chinese name cards are often printed with Chinese on one side and English on the other. Match the two sides of the following name cards.

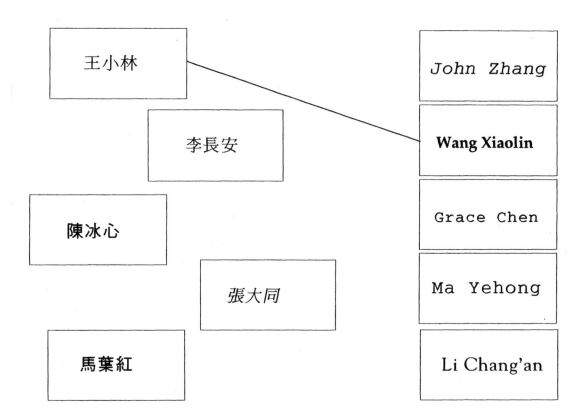

4. Match the traditional to the simplified characters.

我們　　　　　　　陳

你們　　　　　　　我们

他們　　　　　　　谁

誰　　　　　　　　什么

甚麼　　　　　　　他们

陳　　　　　　　　马

馬　　　　　　　　你们

5. Summary. For each word in English, fill in the *pinyin*, the corresponding number for traditional characters and the corresponding letter for simplified characters.

surname			
first name			
sex			
we			
you (plural)			
they			
Zhang (Chang)			
Wang (Wong)			
Li (Lee)			
Ma			
Chen			
what			
who			
to be called			
to be			

1. 張		a. 叫	
2. 性別		b. 我们	
3. 姓		c. 李	
4. 叫		d. 什么	
5. 他們		e. 是	
6. 李		f. 王	
7. 我們		g. 姓	
8. 是		h. 名	
9. 陳		i. 张	
10. 甚麼		j. 谁	
11. 名		k. 马	
12. 王		l. 你们	
13. 你們		m. 性別	
14. 誰		n. 陈	
15. 馬		o. 他们	

6. Practice writing.

字 子 zì word, character

們 们 人 men (plural marker)

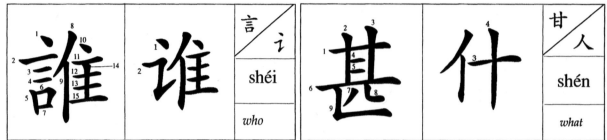

誰 谁 言 讠 shéi who

甚 什 甘 人 shén what

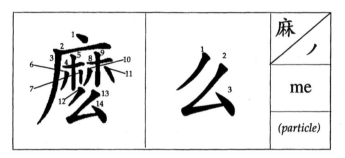

麼 么 麻 丿 me (particle)

7. Write your own name in characters and *pinyin*.

☐ ☐ ☐

8. Fill in the blanks on the form below, using characters for the ones on the first line and English for the rest.

姓　　　　　名

性別　　　　國籍　　　　生年

SEGMENT B: Social titles.

1. Read aloud with a partner.

Two neighbors, a man and a woman, meet at the bus-stop.

陳：馬女士，您好嗎？　　　　Ms. Ma, how are you?

馬：好，好。你呢？　　　　　Fine, fine. And you?

陳：很好。　　　　　　　　　I'm fine.

馬：陳太太呢？　　　　　　　How is Mrs. Chen?

陳：她也很好，謝謝。　　　　She's fine too, thank you.

They part. Ma later runs into a friend of hers.

馬：老張！　　　　　　　　　Zhang! (Old Zhang!)

張：小李！你好嗎？　　　　　Li! (Young Li!) How are you?

馬：我不姓李。　　　　　　　My name isn't Li.

　　我姓馬。　　　　　　　　My name is Ma.

張：對不起，對不起。　　　　Sorry, sorry.

　　馬小姐，你好。　　　　　Miss Ma, hello.

2. Below are five envelopes for hand-delivered invitations. Rain has washed out two characters.
Draw lines matching the envelopes to the invitation list on the left.

Key: 女 = female. 男 = male. 已婚 = married. 未婚 = not (yet) married.

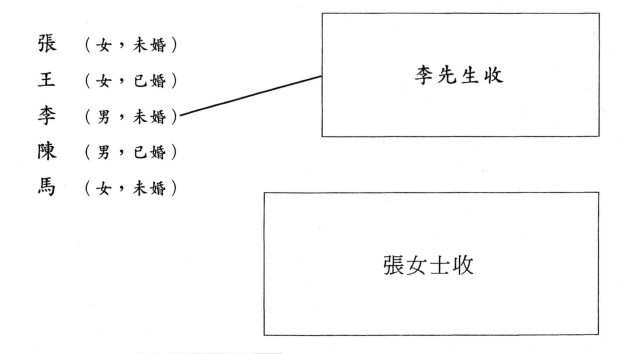

張　（女，未婚）
王　（女，已婚）
李　（男，未婚）
陳　（男，已婚）
馬　（女，未婚）

李先生收

張女士收

馬小姐收

●太太收

●
先
生
收

3. This is an envelope from a hotel in Beijing, addressed for hand-delivery to a guest.

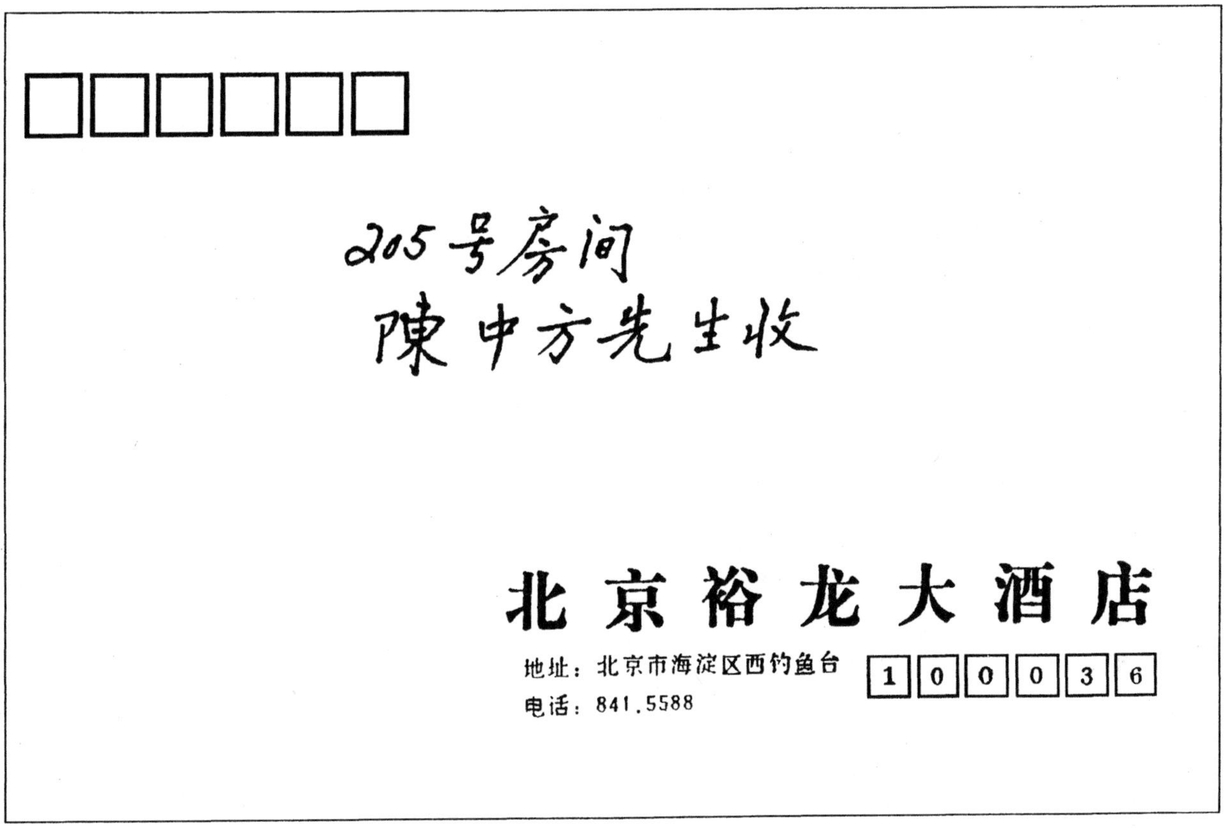

□ □ □ □ □ □

205 号房间
陈中方先生收

北 京 裕 龙 大 酒 店
地址：北京市海淀区西钓鱼台   1 0 0 0 3 6
电话：841.5588

• Circle and label the title given the addressee.

• *X shōu* means "to be received by X." Draw a circle around the character for *shōu*.

4. This is an envelope addressed for delivery through the mail.

•Circle and label the recipient's name.

•Circle and label the recipient's title.

•Circle and label the recipient's address.

•Is the recipient male or female? (Circle one.)

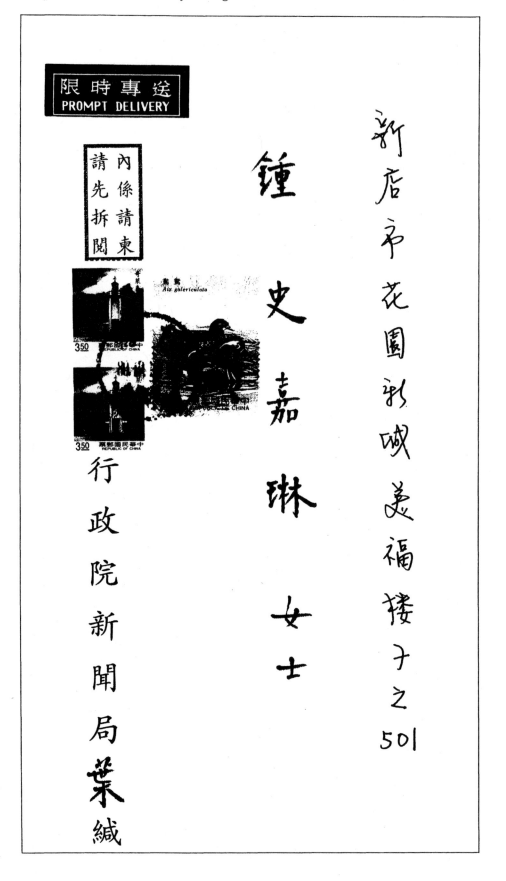

5. Summary. For each word in English, fill in the *pinyin*, the corresponding number for traditional characters and the corresponding letter for simplified characters.

Ms.			
Mr.			
Mrs.			
Miss			
Young X			
Old X			
How about X?			
also (+ a verb)			
to receive			
sorry			

1. 太太	a. 女士
2. 小	b. 对不起
3. 先生	c. 小姐
4. 也	d. 小
5. 收	e. 老
6. 女士	f. 也
7. 老	g. 呢
8. 呢	h. 太太
9. 小姐	i. 先生
10. 對不起	j. 收

6. Practice writing.

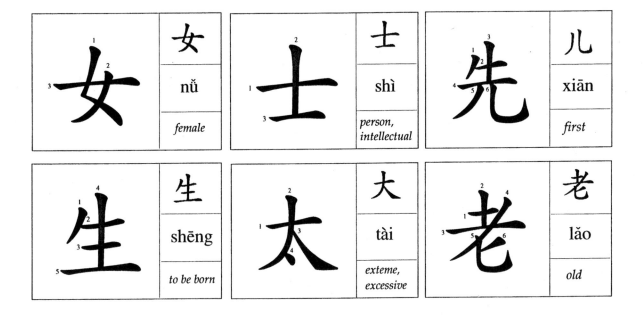

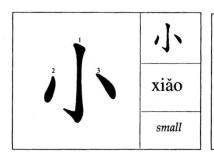

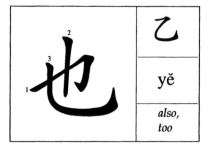

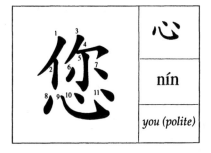

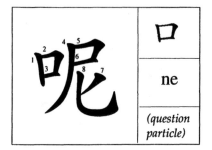

7. Address these envelopes for hand-delivery to two people in your class—one male and one female. Use their Chinese last name and give them a title.

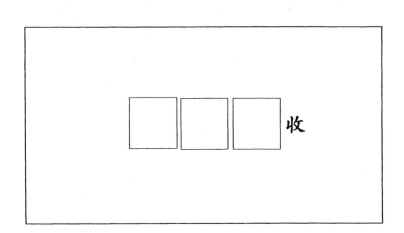

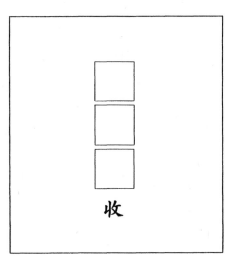

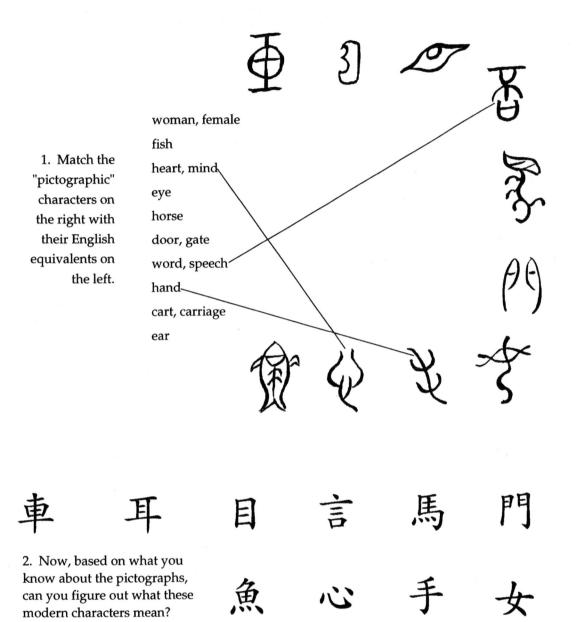

1. Match the "pictographic" characters on the right with their English equivalents on the left.

woman, female

fish

heart, mind

eye

horse

door, gate

word, speech

hand

cart, carriage

ear

2. Now, based on what you know about the pictographs, can you figure out what these modern characters mean?

車   耳   目   言   馬   門

魚   心   手   女

3. Label each character in item 2 above with one of the following identifications.

yán (word, speech)   mén (door, gate)   mǎ (horse)   ěr (ear)   mù (eye)

chē (cart, carriage)   shǒu (hand)   xīn (heart, mind)   yú (fish)   nǚ (woman, female)

4. Circle the radicals you recognize in the following characters.

駕 to ride	旦 dawn, day	語 language	好 good
駛 to drive	映 shine, reflect	話 speech	姦 treacherous
駿 fleet-footed, swift	晚 evening, night	盲 blind	眼 eye
鮮 fresh	閂 door latch	軌 a rut, an orbit	聲 sound
鯊 a shark	開 to open	輛 chariot, cart	聽 to listen

5. Some radicals are altered when they combine with another character component. Match the full forms on the left below with the combination form on the right.

手

心

忄

扌

6. Circle the radicals in the following characters.

打   扔   推   拉

to hit, beat   to throw   to push   to pull

性   怕   悲   忘

nature, temperament   to be afraid   to be sad, melancholic   to forget

7. Try to pick out the radicals in the characters below.

問   排   講   悅   聊

請   婆   鯨   睡   魯

耶   拿   關   嫁   怎

輩   恐   輕   鯉   驚

托   馮   軍   奶   閨

看   誰   妙   眉   聖

8. Write the radicals, following the stroke order indicated.

SEGMENT C: Personal descriptions

Q: 你覺得我們好看嗎？

1. Check one of the three responses given for each picture below. Predict
which response your neighbor will check, then see if your prediction was right.

A: 很好看 ☐
不好看 ☐
很 難看 ☐

A: 很好看 ☐
不好看 ☐
很 難看 ☐

Q: 你覺得我們好看嗎？

2. Check any of the following you think is appropriate.

A： 你很好看。 ☐

你很高。 ☐

你很白。 ☐

你不白，很黑。 ☐

你不好看。 ☐

你很難看。 ☐

Which ones do you think your neighbor checked? Make a prediction; then see if you are right.

Guess what this simplified character term means.

难看 _____

3. Read aloud with a partner.

Ma and Wang are best friends. Ma is having an anxiety attack.

馬： 我很難看。	I'm ugly (unattractive).
王： 不，你不難看。	No, you're not ugly.
馬： 小王很好看。	Wang is very nice-looking.
王： 是嗎？	Is she?
馬： 是的。她很美。	Yes. She's beautiful.

王：	她很高。	She's tall.
馬：	高好啊。	Tall is better.
王：	也很黑。	And dark.
馬：	黑也好啊。	Dark is better too.
王：	你呢？你也很高，很黑。	How about you? You are also tall and dark.
馬：	我很難看。	I'm ugly.

4. Summary. For each word in English, fill in the *pinyin*, the corresponding number for traditional characters and the corresponding letter for simplified characters.

to be tall			
to be fair			
to be dark			
to be beautiful			
to be good-looking			
to be unattractive			
very			

1. 白   a. 很
2. 好看   b. 难看
3. 難看   c. 黑
4. 高   d. 白
5. 很   e. 美
6. 黑   f. 好看
7. 美   g. 高

5. Practice writing.

白 bái — *to be white, fair*

黑 hēi — *to be black, dark*

高 gāo — *to be tall*

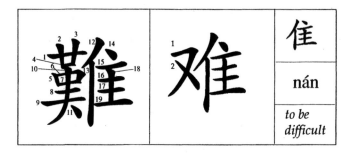

6. Write a statement about your personal appearance. Provide as many details as you can.

SEGMENT D: Age, year/grade, address, telephone number.

1. This is part of a form printed in the US for Chinese immigrants, which has been completed by a middle-aged resident. Match the *pinyin* provided with the characters indicated by writing the appropriate numbers in the bubbles.

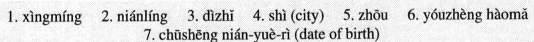

1. xìngmíng   2. niánlíng   3. dìzhǐ   4. shì (city)   5. zhōu   6. yóuzhèng hàomǎ
7. chūshēng nián-yuè-rì (date of birth)

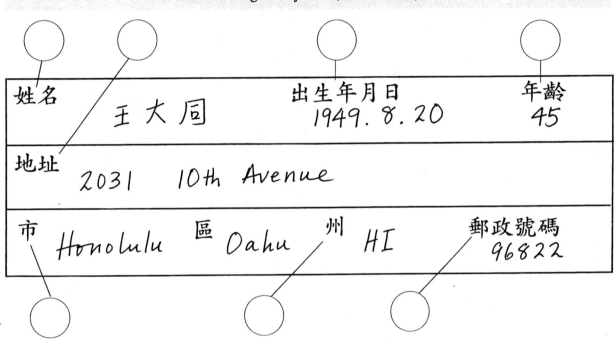

姓名   王大同   出生年月日   年龄
                        1949. 8. 20   45

地址   2031   10th Avenue

市   Honolulu   區   Oahu   州   HI   郵政號碼
                                          96822

2. These are the front and back views of a single name card.

- Fill in the telephone numbers in the English version.
- Circle and label the Chinese words for "address" and "telephone."

山东大学中文系教授

元世硕

地址：：济南市山东大学中文系
电话：：四三八六一——二三四二
四五九六一

Shandong University • Department of Chinese

Professor

Yuan Shishuo

Address: Dept. of Chinese, Shandong University, Jinan

Tel: _____

_____ — _____

3. These signs mark two streets in Beijing.

•Circle the character lù meaning "road."

•Circle the two characters meaning "grand avenue."

4. On the opposite page is a self-addressed survey card issued by a bus company in Taiwan. It asks the recipient to identify him/herself on this side, and on the reverse (not reproduced here) asks further questions regarding bus service.

• The card is addressed to the bus company. Circle and label the three-digit zip code in the address.

• The card is being directed to P.O. Box 53. Circle and label the three characters wŭ sān hào.

• Circle and label the name of the addressee—"Dayou Bus Company Ltd. (Passenger Service Center)."

• Circle the character shōu, meaning "to be received by."

• Circle and label the following items.

Name:

Sex: ☐ male
     ☐ female

Age: *(niánlíng)*

Occupation:

Telephone:

Address: *(zhùzhǐ; synonym for dìzhǐ)*

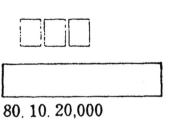

台北郵政第四八之五三號信箱

105

大有巴士股份有限公司（乘客服務中心）收

姓名：

性別：☐男 ☐女

年齡：

職業：

住址：

電話：

廣　告　回　信

台灣北區郵政管理局登記證

北台字第　1445　號

80. 10. 20,000

5. Read aloud with a partner.

Situation 1

Wang chats with a child on a playground.

王：	你幾歲了？	How old are you?
小美：	六歲。	Six.
王：	你念幾年級？	What grade are you in?
小美：	一年級。	First grade.

Situation 2

A asks B for directions.

甲：十路在哪兒？		Where is 10th Street?
乙：在那兒。		Over there.

Situation 3

Chen and Li have just become acquainted in a class they have together.

陳：你的電話號碼是 多少？		What is your telephone number?
李：七八八九五四九。		788-9549.
陳：你的地址呢？		How about your address?
李：五街九三二號，		932 Fifth Avenue,
八六七室。		Apartment 867.

6. Scan through the following message, then do the tasks on the following page.

老張：
　　王呈來電話了。他讓你給他
回個電話。他的電話號碼是65-6510。

　　　　　　　　　　　陳美

• The note was written by _____ to _____. It mentions a third party named _____.

                a. Lao Zhang   b. Wang Xing   c. Chen Mei

• What precipitates this message?

Lao Zhang had a   □   male visitor.

                        □   female visitor.

                        □   phone call from a woman.

                        □   phone call from a man.

• What do the numbers in the text signify? _____

7. Match the simplified to the traditional characters.

歲
年
級
號
碼
號
電
話
幾
哪
兒

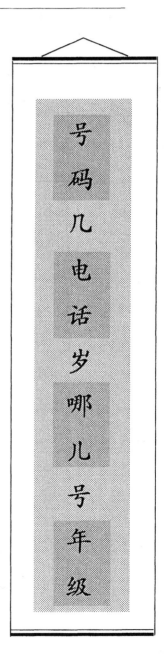

号
碼
几
电
话
岁
哪
儿
号
年
级

8. Summary. For each word in English, fill in the *pinyin* , the corresponding number for traditional characters and the corresponding letter for simplified characters.

birth	chūshēng		
date	nián-yuè-rì		
age	niánlíng		
address			
city			
street	jiē		
road	lù		
zip code	yóuzhèng hàomǎ		
telephone			
number			
occupation	zhíyè		
which grade	jǐ niánjí		
Where is it?			
what number			
years (of age)	suì		

1. 路
2. 號碼
3. 郵政號碼
4. 市
5. 幾年級
6. 在哪兒？
7. 出生
8. 年齡
9. 歲
10. 職業
11. 年月日
12. 街
13. 多少號
14. 電話
15. 地址

a. 市
b. 在哪儿？
c. 职业
d. 年龄
e. 路
f. 街
g. 年月日
h. 几年级
i. 电话
j. 邮政号码
k. 多少号
l. 地址
m. 号码
n. 岁
o. 出生

9. Practice writing.

街	行 jiē — street, avenue	
路	足 lù — road	
在	土 zài — to be at	
多	夕 duō — many, much	
少	小 shǎo — few	
的	白 de — (particle)	

電	电	雨 / 乚 diàn — electric, electricity
話	话	言 huà — language, speech
幾	几	幺 / 几 jǐ — how many
歲	岁	止 / 山 suì — year (of age)
級	级	糸 jí — grade, rank
兒	儿	儿 ér — child, son; (suffix)

10. Fill in the blanks in the following table with information about yourself. Write characters when you can; when you cannot, use *pinyin* and/or English.

姓名	性別 ☐男 ☐女	出生年月日	年齡
電話號碼	地址		
市	區	州	郵政號碼

11. Begin writing a brief self-introduction in characters. (You will continue in subsequent chapters.) Include information about your **name, age, telephone number, and address.**

12. Check the statement that applies to you. Fill in the blank as appropriate.

☐ 我念大學 (college) _____年級。

☐ 我念高中 (high school) _____ 年級。

☐ 我是研究生 (graduate student)。

☐ 我不是學生 (student)。

SEGMENT E: Height, weight, birthday.

1. Fill in the blanks with your personal information, using Arabic numerals. ➡

我 ＿＿尺＿＿寸高。
(Fill in your height in the English system.)

我 ＿＿米＿＿＿。
(Fill in your height in the metric system.)

我 ＿＿磅。
(Fill in your weight in the English system.)

我 ＿＿公斤。
(Fill in your weight in the metric system.)

我 ＿＿斤。
(Fill in your weight in the Chinese system.)

2. Fill in the blanks with your personal information. ⬇

我生日是 ＿＿＿＿＿＿＿＿年 ＿＿月 ＿＿日。

(Fill in the year, month, and day of your birthday.)

3. This is a ticket stub to a tourist attraction in China.

• What is the height in metres at which children must also purchase a ticket?

＿＿＿＿＿＿＿

参 观 须 知

1. 请勿携带易燃，易爆物品入内。

2. 爱护古建请勿涂写刻画，请勿抚摸文物展品。

3. 殿内请勿摄影，请勿吸烟，请勿随地吐痰。

4. 一米二以上儿童照章购票。

5. 每券只限一人。票价：0.50元。

4. Read aloud with a partner.
Zhang and Li are new room-mates. Zhang is Chinese and Li is Chinese-American.

李：	你有多高？	How tall are you?
張：	我一米八。你呢？	I'm 1.8 metres. And you?
李：	我五尺六寸。 那是一米六八。	I'm 5 feet 6 inches. That's 1.68 metres.
張：	你有多重？ 有一百公斤嗎？	How heavy are you? Are you 100 kilograms?

李： 一公斤是幾磅？　　　　　　How many pounds are in a kilogram?

張： 一公斤是二點二磅。　　　　A kilogram is 2.2 pounds.

李： 我沒有一百公斤。　　　　　I'm not 100 kilograms.

　　　我是一百九十磅。　　　　　I'm 190 pounds.

　　　你的生日是幾月幾號？　　　When is your birthday?

張： 十一月二十八號。　　　　　November 28th.

5. This is the top portion of a Taiwan health clinic's patient information form.

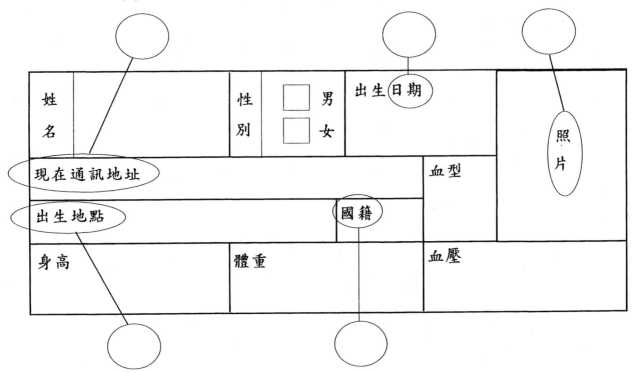

• Match the items below to the categories circled by writing the appropriate numbers in the bubbles.

　　　1. guójí (nationality)

　　　2. rìqī (same as 年月日)

　　　3. xiànzài tōngxùn dìzhǐ (current mailing address)

　　　4. zhàopiàn (photograph)

　　　5. chūshēng dìdiǎn (place of birth)

• Fill in your name, gender, date of birth, nationality, current mailing address, height and weight in the appropriate spaces on the form. Write characters when you can.

6. Have available highlighter pens in three colors for this item.

The following personal advertisement from a PRC magazine consists of three sections.

• The first two sentences describe the person placing the ad. Highlight these in color 1.

• The next sentence (beginning with the character 觅) describes the person sought. Highlight this in color 2.

• The rest of the ad is information about how to contact the person who placed the ad. Highlight this in color 3.

• Provide the information indicated.

> ● 男，26岁，高1。75米，助工，诚实，善良，重感情，爱生活。品正貌佳，经济好，家有住房。觅中专以上，高1。60米左右，正派，温柔，善良，25岁以下的本市女子为侣。有意者信照寄北京东单八宝楼胡同4号杨桂玲。邮码:100005。

Section 1: Advertiser	Section 2: Person sought	Section 3: Address
Gender	Gender	Name of advertiser
Age	Approximate height	Street number
Height	Maximum age	Zip code

7. Summary. For each word in English, fill in the *pinyin*, the corresponding number for traditional characters and the corresponding letter for simplified characters.

foot			
inch			
metre			
pound			
kilogram			
<u>jin</u> (catty)			
birthday			
what date			
how tall			
height			
weight			
photograph	*zhàopiàn*		
nationality			

1. 斤　　　　　　a. 照片
2. 身高　　　　　b. 寸
3. 幾月幾日　　　c. 多高
4. 照片　　　　　d. 米
5. 生日　　　　　e. 体重
6. 多高　　　　　f. 身高
7. 體重　　　　　g. 公斤
8. 寸　　　　　　h. 磅
9. 尺　　　　　　i. 斤
10. 米　　　　　　j. 尺
11. 國籍　　　　　k. 生日
12. 磅　　　　　　l. 几月几日
13. 公斤　　　　　m. 国籍

8. Practice writing.

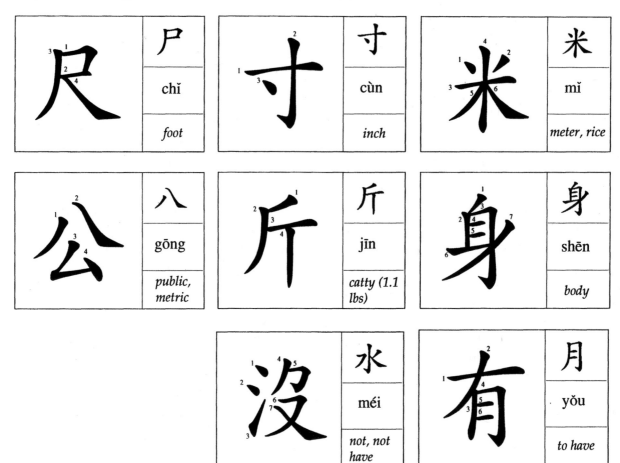

9. Continue your self-introduction. Include information on your height, weight, and birthday.

SEGMENT F: Professions.

1. Write *pinyin* in the blanks below.

2. On the following page is an excerpt from a Taipei McDonald's placemat. ➡

  •Circle and label the two occurences of the term fúwùyuán (waitperson, clerk, attendant).

  • Circle and label the two occurences of the term jīnglǐ (manager).

  •The theme of this ad is "My future is not a dream."
        Circle and label "my" (wǒde).
        Circle and label "future" (wèilái).
        Circle and label "dream" (mèng).
        This theme is echoed in the small print. Find where.

  •"McDonald's" is transliterated "Màidāngláo." Circle and label three occurences of these three characters.

3. Match the captions to the photographs below.

店員在吸煙。 [ ]

小女孩兒在看警察。 [ ]

A

B

訓練員

服務員

服務員

訓練員

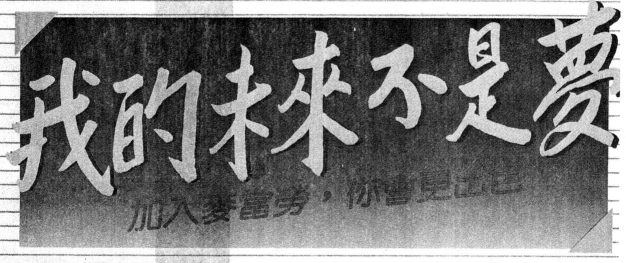

我的未來不是夢

加入麥當勞，你會更出色

中心經理

加入麥當勞你立刻擁有符合你所需
求的基本福利──

● 彈性上班時間
● 享勞保、供制服、供餐飲
● 完整的訓練計劃，加強個人的競
　爭優勢
● 暢通的升遷管道在麥當勞前程萬
　里，你的未來不是夢。

意者請洽本中心值班經理

McDonald's 麥當勞

中心經理

4. Read aloud with a partner.

Situation 1

A patient approaches an employee of a health clinic.

甲：　請問，您是醫生嗎？　　　　May I ask if you are a doctor?

乙：　不。我是護士。　　　　　　No. I'm a nurse.
　　　　醫生在那兒。　　　　　　The doctor is over there.

Situation 2

The teacher enters at the beginning of an elementary school class.

老師：同學們好。　　　　　　　Hello, students.

學生們：老師好！　　　　　　　Hello, teacher!

Situation 3

Some business people gather at the start of a meeting.

甲：　李先生，您是律師嗎？　　Mr. Li, are you a lawyer?

乙：　不。黃女士是律師。　　　No. Ms. Huang is the lawyer.
　　　　我是秘書。　　　　　　I'm a secretary.

Situation 4

A crowd is gathered at the scene of a fight in a store.

甲：你是服務員嗎？　　　　　　Are you the clerk?

乙：不是。　　　　　　　　　　No.

甲：我是警察。誰是服務員？　　I'm a police officer. Who is the clerk?

丙：我是服務員。　　　　　　　I am the clerk.

5. Match the simplified to the traditional characters.

學生　　　護士　　　醫生　　　秘書　　　服務員　　　店員

護士　　服務員　　店員　　秘書　　學生　　醫生

6. Summary. For each word in English, fill in the *pinyin*, the corresponding number for traditional characters, and the corresponding letter for simplified characters.

English	pinyin		
to grow up	*zhǎng dà*		
doctor			
nurse			
secretary			
lawyer			
teacher			
student			
clerk, waiter			
manager	*jīnglǐ*		
to do, to be	*zuò*		
May I ask...			
classmate	*tóngxué*		
store clerk	*diànyuán*		

1. 請問
2. 做
3. 老師
4. 醫生
5. 秘書
6. 服務員
7. 學生
8. 護士
9. 同學
10. 律師
11. 經理
12. 店員
13. 長大

a. 老师
b. 经理
c. 服务员
d. 律师
e. 店员
f. 学生
g. 长大
h. 做
i. 护士
j. 秘书
k. 医生
l. 同学
m. 请问

7. Practice writing.

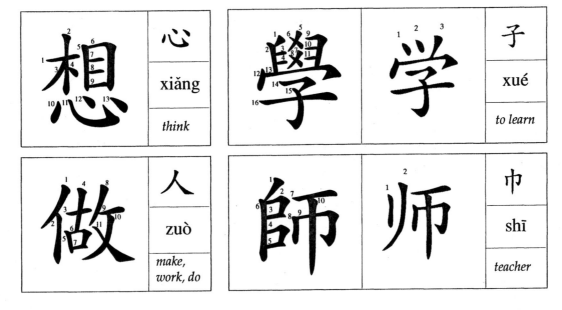

想 心 xiǎng think

學 學 子 xué to learn

做 人 zuò make, work, do

師 师 巾 shī teacher

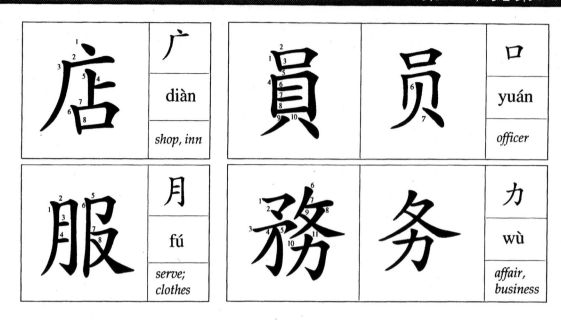

广 diàn shop, inn	店	员 yuán officer	員
月 fú serve; clothes	服	力 wù affair, business	务 務

8. Pretend that you are a teacher, a store clerk, or a wait person, and fill out this form completely.

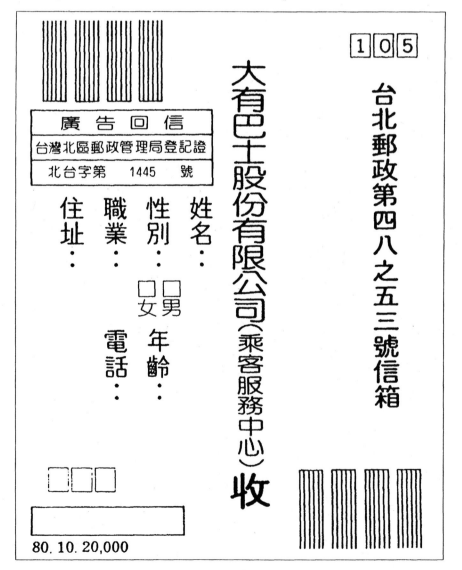

台北郵政第四八之五三號信箱

105

廣　告　回　信
台灣北區郵政管理局登記證
北台字第　1445　號

大有巴士股份有限公司(乘客服務中心)收

姓名：

性別：□男　□女

職業：　年齡：

住址：　電話：

80. 10. 20,000

SEGMENT G: Nationality and foreign language.

1. Following are two signs in Beijing.

"American Consulate General. This way."

• Circle "America."

• "This way" is yóu cǐ qù in literary Chinese. Circle this phrase.

"Long Live the People's Republic of China."

• Circle the characters zhōng and guó that combine to make "China."

• "X wàn suì" (literally "10,000 years of age") means "Long live X." Circle wàn suì.

2. Match the stamps to the names of the countries, as appropriate. (Not all matches are one-to-one; not all items can be matched.)

3. This is a list of country codes for international long distance calls, provided by a hotel in the PRC.

国际直拨电话号码及收费：		
国家／地区	国家／地区代号	每分钟费用
美国	001	10.00
意大利	0039	18.00
英国	0044	18.00
德国	0049	18.00
澳大利亚	0061	18.00
新加坡	0065	15.00
日本	0081	11.00
香港	00852	10.00
台湾	00886	10.00

• Please write the country codes for the following countries:

USA: _____

England: _____

Germany: _____

Japan: _____

• Two of the unmatched stamps on the previous page are from Yìdàlì and Àodàlìyà. Find the characters for these names, circle them, and label them with their English equivalents.

• Circle and label Xiānggǎng as Hong Kong.

• Circle and label Táiwān.

• The last remaining name is Xīnjiāpō. You'll find this city-state represented among the stamps on the previous page. Circle the characters and label them with their English equivalents.

4. Read aloud with a partner.

Situation 1

Zhang and Wang are new colleagues meeting at the beginning of a semester.

張： 你會說哪國話？ What languages can you speak?

王： 中文、英文、 Chinese, English, French.

法國話。你呢？ How about you?

張： 我只會說中文。 I can only speak Chinese.

<u>Situation 2</u>　*Two incoming graduate students meet at a reception.*

陳：俄語難學嗎？　　　　　　　Is Russian hard to learn?

李：不。西班牙話難學。　　　　No. Spanish is hard to learn.

陳：日語呢？　　　　　　　　　How about Japanese?

李：我不會說日語。　　　　　　I can't speak Japanese.

5. Summary. For each word in English, fill in the *pinyin* , the corresponding number for traditional characters and the corresponding letter for simplified characters.

United States			
China			
People's Republic of China			
Republic of China			
"Long live..."	...wàn suì		
Korea			
Japan			
India			
S. E. Asia			
England			
France			
Russia			
Germany			
Spain			
Italy	Yìdàlì		
Australia	Àodàlìyǎ		
Hong Kong	Xiānggǎng		
Taiwan	Táiwān		
Singapore	Xīnjiāpō		
English			
Japanese	Rìyǔ		
Hindi			

1. 法國　　　　a. 西班牙
2. 德國　　　　b. 台湾
3. 西班牙　　　c. 俄国
4. 英國　　　　d. 印度语
5. 中國　　　　e. 东南亚
6. 俄國　　　　f. 英国
7. 新加坡　　　g. 意大利
8. 中華民國　　h. 日语
9. 美國　　　　i. 英文
10. 台灣　　　　j. 香港
11. 萬歲　　　　k. 德国
12. 日語　　　　l. 中华人民
　　　　　　　　　共和国
13. 印度語　　　m. 澳大利亚
14. 印度　　　　n. 韩国
15. 澳大利亞　　o. 新加坡
16. 東南亞　　　p. 日本
17. 英文　　　　q. 中华民国
18. 韓國　　　　r. 印度
19. 日本　　　　s. 法国
20. 意大利　　　t. 万岁
21. 香港　　　　u. 美国
22. 中華人民　　v. 中国
　　共和國

6. Practice writing.

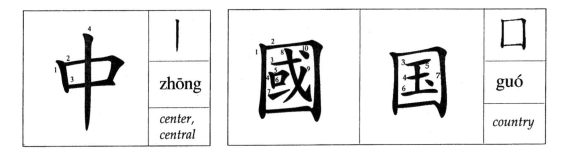

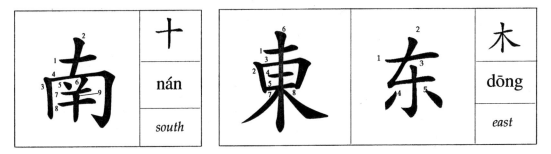

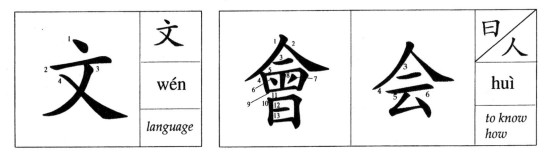

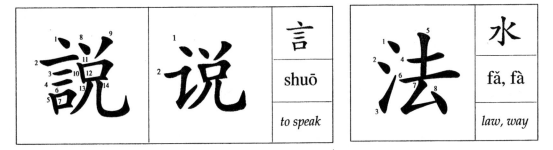

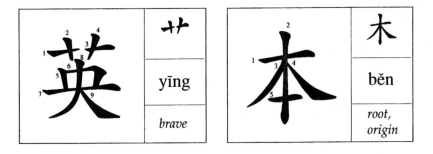

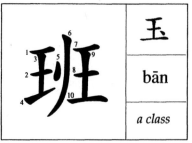

	西
西	xī
	west

	玉
班	bān
	a class

	牙
牙	yá
	tooth

7. Fill in the blanks with information about yourself.

我是 ＿＿＿ 國人。

我會說 ＿＿＿＿＿。

我想學 ＿＿＿＿＿。

8. Now copy the sentences over again, to continue your self -introduction.

SEGMENT H: Family members.

1. Fill in the *pinyin* for the terms indicated, using the photograph as a guide.

爸
爸 _____   哥
哥 _____

姐
姐 _____      弟
弟 _____

妹　媽
_____ 妹　媽 _____

2. According to this message, what is John to do? _____

• The verb in this message is huí (to return). Circle and label it.

• Jí rì means "this day (today)." Circle and label it.

• Can you make out the name of the person who wrote the note? Write the *pinyin.*

John:

请给你妈儿回个电话。

即日

李明

3. This self-introduction was written in 1993 by the holder of the simulated passport below. Highlight all the portions that you can read and understand.

UNITED STATES OF AMERICA

PASSPORT NO.

120203456

Surname
  YU
Given names
  ROBYN XIUMING
Nationality
  United States of America
Date of birth
  15 AUGUST, 1981
Sex   Place of Birth
  F   HAWAII, U.S.A
Date of issue   Date of expiration
  13 FEB 91   12 FEB 96

P<USAYU<<ROBYN<XIUMING<<<<<<<<<<<<<<<<<<<<<<<<<<<<<<<<<<<<<<<<<<<<<<

我 的 英 文 名 字 叫 Robyn.

我 的 中 文 名 字 是 余 修 明.

我 十 二 歲 了. 我 是 女 孩 子.

我 沒 有 哥 哥 姐 姐 弟 弟 妹 妹.

我 會 説 一 點 中 文, 也 會 寫

一 點 中 文. 我 英 文 説

得 很 好.

4. Read the following letter written by an American to a Chinese pen-friend, with the help of the notes provided.

亲爱的笔友：

你好！谢谢你的来信[1]。我想我们将来[2]一定会[3]成为很好的朋友[5]。你说对不对？[6]我来介绍一下[8]我自己[9]和我的家人吧[12]。我有父亲和母亲，可是他们不住在[14]一起[15]。我爸爸住西班牙，妈妈住在美国。我只有一个姐姐，她是一个大夫的[16]秘书，她的爱人[17]是一位工人[18]。他们有两个孩子[19]，一个三岁的儿子[20]，一个一岁[21]半的女儿[22]。我三十岁了，住在夏威夷[23]，在大学里[24]教汉语[25]。我有爱人，可是没有孩子。好，我不多写了[26]，请你给我写信[27]告诉我[28]你和你家人的情况[29]。祝[30]

秋安[31]。

朋友[32]

斯地芬[32]九十三年十月十三日上[33]

1. lái xìn — (incoming) letter
2. jiānglái — in the future
3. yídìng — certainly
4. huì chéng wéi — will become
5. péngyou — friends
6. Nǐ shuō duì bú duì? — Don't you think so?
7. wǒ lái — let me
8. jièshào yíxià — just introduce
9. wǒ zìjǐ — myself
10. hé — and
11. wǒ de jiārén — my family
12. ba — particle of suggestion
13. kěshì — but
14. zhù — to live
15. yìqǐ — together
16. zhǐ yǒu — to have only
17. àirén — spouse (PRC usage)
18. yí wèi gōngrén — a worker
19. liǎng ge háizi — two children
20. érzi — son
21. yí suì bàn — a year and a half in age
22. nǚ'ér — daughter
23. Xiàwēiyí — Hawaii
24. dàxuéli — in college
25. jiāo Hànyǔ — teach Chinese
26. Wǒ bù duō xiě le. — I'll stop here. (lit: I won't write any more.)
27. gěi wǒ xiě xìn — write to me
28. gàosu — to tell
29. qíngkuàng — situation
30. zhù — to wish
31. qiū ān — a happy autumn season
32. Sīdìfēn — Stephen
33. shàng — "respectfully presents you this letter"

5. Summary. For each word in English, fill in the *pinyin*, the corresponding number for traditional characters and the corresponding letter for simplified characters.

family	*jiārén*		
father	*fùqīn*		
dad, papa			
mother	*mǔqīn*		
mom, mama			
older brother			
younger brother			
older sister			
younger sister			
siblings	*xiōngdì jiěmèi*		
spouse (PRC)			
child			
daughter			
son			
girl	*nǚ háizi*		
boy	*nán háizi*		
Dear X...	*Qīn'àide*		

1. 兒子
2. 母親
3. 家人
4. 哥哥
5. 親愛的
6. 女兒
7. 弟弟
8. 姐姐
9. 爸爸
10. 愛人
11. 媽媽
12. 女孩子
13. 男孩子
14. 兄弟姐妹
15. 妹妹
16. 父親
17. 孩子

a. 爸爸
b. 女儿
c. 哥哥
d. 女孩子
e. 妈妈
f. 兄弟姐妹
g. 姐姐
h. 男孩子
i. 妹妹
j. 儿子
k. 父亲
l. 亲爱的
m. 孩子
n. 母亲
o. 爱人
p. 家人
q. 弟弟

6. Practice writing.

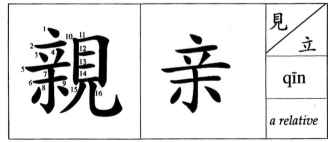

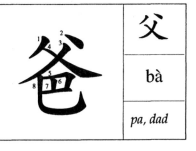

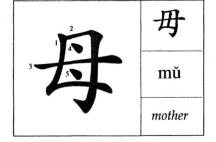
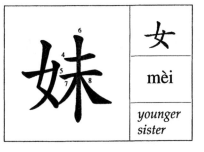

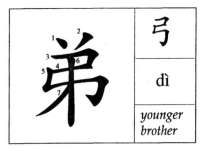

7. Fill in the blanks below (in characters!), based on the English.

<u>Situation 1</u>

Two people are getting acquainted.

甲：你有＿＿＿＿＿＿＿嗎？　　　　Do you have brothers & sisters?

乙：我只有兩＿＿＿＿＿妹妹。　　　I only have two younger sisters.

甲：她們住在＿＿＿＿＿？　　　　　Where do they live?

乙：她們都＿＿＿＿＿美國。　　　　They both live in the US.

<u>Situation 2</u>

An older man chats with a young father at a bus-stop.

甲：　你的兒子幾 ＿＿＿＿＿＿ 了？　　How old is your son?

乙：　不是兒子，是 ＿＿＿＿＿＿ 。　　It's not a son, it's a daughter.
　　　兩歲了。　　　　　　　　　　　　　She's two.

<u>Situation 3</u>

A Chinese student and an American student are studying together.

中國學生：中國人一般説

　　　　『＿＿＿＿＿＿＿＿』。　　Chinese generally say "east-south-west-north." That's not how the Americans say it, is it?

　　　美國人不是這麼説的吧？

美國學生：不。＿＿＿＿＿＿　　No. Americans say "north-south-east-west.

　　　説『＿＿＿＿＿＿』。

8. Respond briefly to 斯地芬's letter in item 4, above, providing your new pen-friend some of the same sort of information he does.

親愛的斯地芬：

＿＿＿＿＿＿＿＿＿＿＿＿

＿＿＿＿＿＿＿＿＿＿＿＿＿＿＿＿

＿＿＿＿＿＿＿＿＿＿＿＿＿＿＿＿

＿＿＿＿＿＿＿＿＿＿＿＿＿＿＿＿

＿＿＿＿＿＿＿＿＿＿＿＿＿＿＿＿

＿＿＿＿＿＿＿＿＿＿＿

朋友 ＿＿＿＿＿＿＿ 上

＿＿ 年 ＿＿ 月 ＿＿ 日

1. Some of the radicals you have seen before have common, colloquial names in Chinese. Match these names on the left with the radicals on the right.

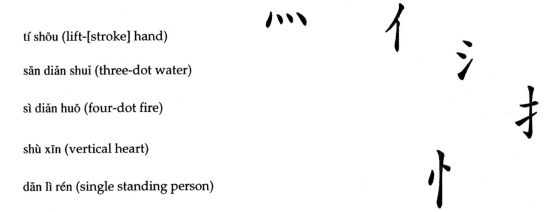

tí shǒu (lift-[stroke] hand)

sān diǎn shuǐ (three-dot water)

sì diǎn huǒ (four-dot fire)

shù xīn (vertical heart)

dān lì rén (single standing person)

2. The colloquial names of the following two radicals are similar to the ones above. Match the names to the radicals.

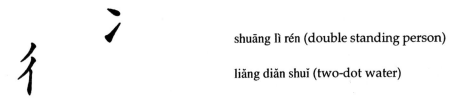

shuāng lì rén (double standing person)

liǎng diǎn shuǐ (two-dot water)

3. Match the combination forms of the radicals below with their full forms in the bottom row.

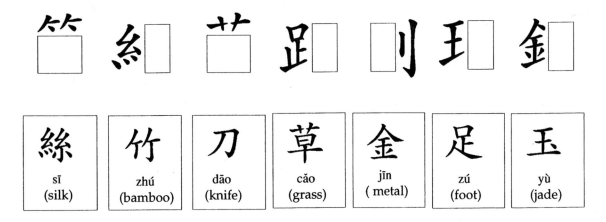

絲	竹	刀	草	金	足	玉
sī (silk)	zhú (bamboo)	dāo (knife)	cǎo (grass)	jīn (metal)	zú (foot)	yù (jade)

4. The two radicals in combination form on the left are matched with the full forms on the right. The combination forms look very similar. Can you spot the differences?

礻 ——————— 示   shì (an omen; to reveal)

衤 ——————— 衣   yī (clothing)

5. Match the colloquial names with the radicals.

yòu ěr dāo (right ear)

zuǒ ěr dāo (left ear)

6. Match the meanings with the radicals.

an enclosure

to run and stop

a roof

7. Circle the radical in each character below, and label it with the corresponding number from the chart.

亻1	²刂	囗3	王4	冫5	金6	礻7
衤8	扌9	忄10	冖11	彳12	竹13	糸14
艹15	足16	阝17	18阝	宀19	灬20	辶21

給　　錢　　花　　裡　　第　　德

玩　　進　　作　　跟　　那　　慢

院　　家　　冷　　遠　　刻　　後

萬　　國　　然　　笑　　宜　　圖

快　　們　　把　　汽　　紙　　祝

SEGMENT A: Physical condition.

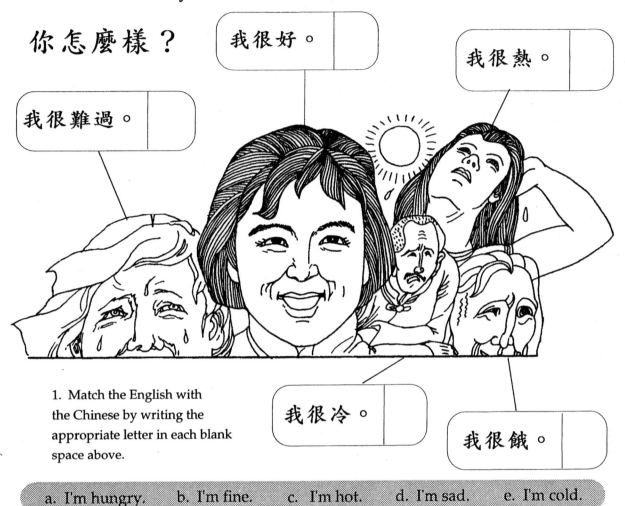

你怎麼樣？

我很好。

我很熱。

我很難過。

我很冷。

我很餓。

1. Match the English with the Chinese by writing the appropriate letter in each blank space above.

a. I'm hungry.   b. I'm fine.   c. I'm hot.   d. I'm sad.   e. I'm cold.

2. Read aloud with a partner.

Situation 1

Zhang and Wang share an office. Zhang sees Wang looking glum.

張： 小王，你累不累？   Wang, are you tired?

王： 我不累。我很忙。   I'm not tired. I'm busy.

Situation 2

A father and son are reading together in the evening.

爸爸：你冷嗎？   Are you cold?

小明：我不冷。   I'm not cold.

爸爸：我有點冷。   I'm a little cold.

Situation 3

Three students are studying together. Chen would like to go to lunch.

陳： 誰餓了嗎？　　　　　　　　Is anyone hungry?

李： 我不餓。有一點渴。　　　　I'm not hungry. I'm a little thirsty.

馬： 我很飽。　　　　　　　　　I'm very full.

陳： 你們都不餓。只有　　　　　You are both not hungry. I'm the
　　 我餓了。　　　　　　　　　only one hungry. (Only I am hun-
　　　　　　　　　　　　　　　　gry.)

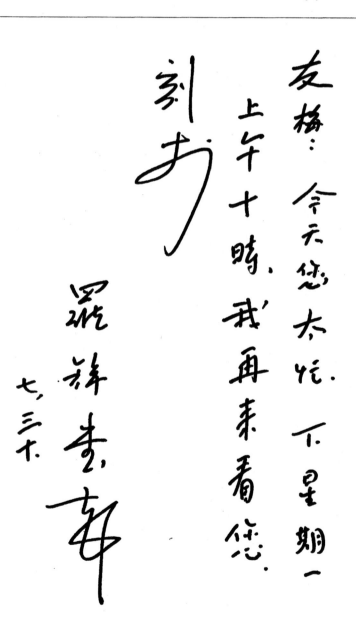

3. "You are too busy today. I'll come back to see you next Monday at 10 a.m."

• Circle and label the words "too busy."

• Circle and label the sentence "I'll come again to see you."

4. NOTES. On the left is a series of notes 小王 received from one of her room-mates over the course of a year. On the right are similar notes received by an American college student. Match the ones most similar in meaning.

我餓了，
先走了。

Have a drink if
you're thirsty.
Check the fridge.

熱死了！

I'm pooped.
Won't go dancing
tonight.

我今晚太累，
不去跳舞了。

Have gone ahead.
Am starving.

你渴嗎？冰箱
裡有汽水。

Still hungry! Went
out to get a burger.

十個餃子吃不飽！我
上街再去吃點兒。

What's with this
HEAT??

5. Summary. For each word in English, fill in the *pinyin*, the corresponding number for traditional characters and the corresponding letter for simplified characters.

How are you doing?			
too cold			
too hot			
too tired			
too busy			
too hungry			
too full			
to leave first			
both, all			

1.太冷   a.太饿

2.太飽   b.太热

3.都   c.先走

4.太累   d.都

5.你怎麼樣？   e.太忙

6.太餓   f.太累

7.太熱   g.你怎么样？

8.先走   h.太饱

9.太忙   i.太冷

6. Practice writing.

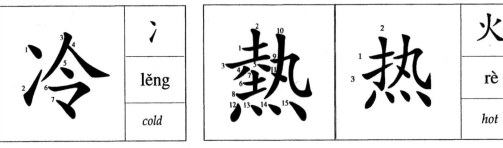

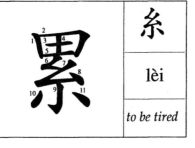

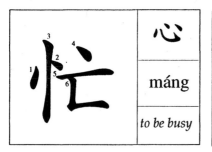

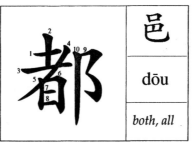

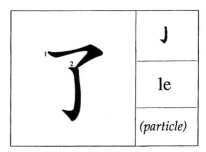

7. Fill in the blanks in the following notes.
Use Chinese characters.

媽：

我 ＿＿＿＿＿ 了。先回去了。

*Mom, I'm tired. I've
gone home first.*

老師：

教室太 ＿＿＿＿＿＿ 了。

學生 ＿＿＿＿＿＿ 上

Teacher, the classroom's too cold.
Your student,
(your name)

小李：

謝謝你。我 ＿＿＿＿＿＿ 了。
你吃吧。

＿＿＿＿＿＿

Li: Thanks, but I'm full. You eat these.
(your name)

8. Write a note telling someone goodbye; you're leaving because you are ＿＿＿＿＿＿ (you choose a reason).

＿＿＿＿＿＿

＿＿＿＿＿＿

＿＿＿＿＿＿

＿＿＿＿＿＿

＿＿＿＿＿＿

SEGMENT B: Personal needs and wants.

1. Guess what this place is.   ➡

Answer: _____

The sign below says "Public

_____

•The word for "public" is gōnggòng. Circle these characters.
•How might gōnggòng cèsuǒ be abbreviated to two characters?

2. Read aloud with a partner.

Situation 1
In a classroom.

老師：陳美英在哪兒？   Where's Chen Meiying?

學生：她上廁所了。   She went to the bathroom.

Situation 2
At home, before bedtime.

媽媽：小妹，你洗澡了嗎？   Little sister, have you taken a bath?

妹妹：洗了。   Yes. (I've bathed.)

媽媽：弟弟呢？   How about little brother?

妹妹：弟弟沒洗。   He hasn't.

Situation 3

A father and son are together in the evening.

爸爸：誰在看電視？　　　　　　　Who's watching television?

小明：沒人看。爸爸，　　　　　　No one's watching. Dad,
　　　我餓了。　　　　　　　　　I'm hungry.

爸爸：那你來吃點兒東西吧。　　　Then come eat something.

Situation 4

At a restaurant.

中國人：你想喝茶嗎？　　　　　　Would you like some tea?

美國人：不，我要喝水。　　　　　No, I'll drink water.
　　　　你喝茶吧。　　　　　　　You have tea.

Situation 5

Two students, out hiking, near a rest point.

女生：我想吃東西。　　　　　　　I feel like eating something.

男生：你吃吧。　　　　　　　　　Go ahead and eat.

女生：你呢？你不吃嗎？　　　　　How about you? Won't you eat?

男生：不。我只要休息休息。　　　No. I just want to rest a while.

Situation 6

In a hospital.

醫生：王女士呢？　　　　　　　　Where's Ms. Wang?

護士：睡覺去了。　　　　　　　　Gone to sleep.

3. NOTES.

明:

快去洗澡
睡覺。不要
再看書看電
視了。

媽

What instructions are given in this note?

Do_____ and _____ .

Don't _____ or _____ .

潘老师:
　　若你明天下午 5:00 有空的话,我
们去北京楼吃饭好吗?
　　　　　　　　　　林
　　　　　　　　　　11月12日

What does 林 propose to do tomorrow afternoon at 5:00?

Answer: _____

4. Summary. For each word in English, fill in the *pinyin*, the corresponding number for traditional characters and the corresponding letter for simplified characters.

women's toilet			
men's toilet			
public restroom			
to use the toilet			
to bathe			
to watch T.V.			
to eat something			
to eat a meal			
to have eaten already			
to drink tea			
to drink water			
to rest			
to sleep			
to read			

1. 洗澡　　　　a. 吃过了
2. 吃東西　　　b. 看书
3. 喝水　　　　c. 男厕
4. 女廁　　　　d. 看电视
5. 公共廁所　　e. 睡觉
6. 吃過了　　　f. 吃东西
7. 休息　　　　g. 上厕所
8. 男廁　　　　h. 公共厕所
9. 上廁所　　　i. 休息
10. 看書　　　　j. 喝茶
11. 吃飯　　　　k. 洗澡
12. 看電視　　　l. 喝水
13. 睡覺　　　　m. 女厕
14. 喝茶　　　　n. 吃饭

5. Practice writing.

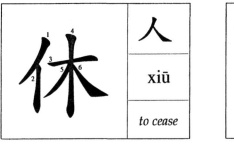

休 | 人 xiū | to cease

息 | 心 xī | to pause

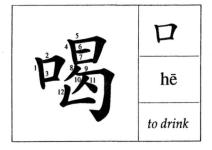

喝 | 口 hē | to drink

茶 | 艹 chá | tea

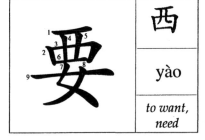

要 | 西 yào | to want, need

水 | 水 shuǐ | water

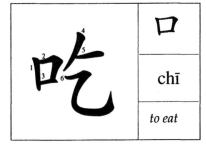

吃 | 口 chī | to eat

飯 饭 | 食 飠 fàn | food, cooked rice

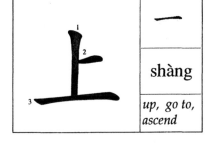

上 | 一 shàng | up, go to, ascend

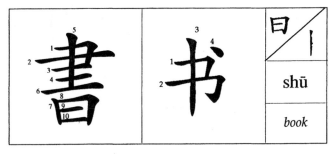

書 书 | 曰 丨 shū | book

6. Fill in each blank with a logical selection from the list provided.
Write in Chinese characters.

我餓了。我想 ＿＿＿＿＿＿＿＿＿。

我渴了。我要 ＿＿＿＿＿＿＿＿＿。

我累了。我想 ＿＿＿＿＿＿＿＿＿。

我不累。我要 ＿＿＿＿＿＿＿＿＿。

看電視　　　吃東西　　　睡覺　　　喝水

7. Write a note telling your friend you are hungry and you went to get something to eat.

＿＿＿＿＿＿＿＿＿

＿＿＿＿＿＿＿＿＿＿＿＿＿＿＿＿＿＿

＿＿＿＿＿＿＿＿＿＿＿＿＿＿＿＿＿＿

＿＿＿＿＿＿＿＿＿＿＿＿＿＿＿＿＿＿

＿＿＿＿＿＿＿＿＿＿＿＿

SEGMENT A: Time by the clock.

• <u>Yíngyè shíjiān</u> means "business hours."

• "# <u>shí</u>" is the literary equivalent of "# <u>diǎn zhōng</u> (#點鐘)." Circle and label the character <u>shí</u>.

• Signs in the PRC and Taiwan often state time by the 24-hour clock. Circle the term "4 p.m."

• "To" (as in "from 9 <u>to</u> 4") in literary Chinese is <u>zhì</u>. Circle and label this character.

1. "OPEN 9 – 4"

營 業 時 間

9 時 至 16 時

This is the sign for a service station at the Taipei airport. What are its hours of operation?

_____

2. Zhang Xueyang is a gentleman of leisure in Shanghai in the 1920s. Terrorists planning to blow up this "bloodsucking scion of the parasitic bourgeoisie" have learned of his daily schedule from a sympathetic household servant. If you were a terrorist planning to eliminate Mr. Zhang during one of the six daily activities listed, at what times would you be waiting for him?

goes shopping   3 p.m.   visits his friend   _____

eats lunch   _____   rests (naps)   _____

bathes   _____   goes to sleep   _____

7時30分	洗澡
8時	吃早餐
8時45分	寫信
9時30分	散步
10時30分	看書
11時30分	吃午飯
12時30分	休息
13時30分	打牌
15時	買東西
16時30分	游泳
17時30分	打球
18時15分	吃晚飯
19時45分	看電視
21時	看朋友
22時	聽音樂
23時	睡覺

安娜：
今天晚上來我家吃便饭，好吗？
我五点半上一路车站接你。
到时候见！

小红

3. What does Xiǎo Hóng invite Anna to do? Answer: _____

When does she suggest they meet? Answer: _____

4. Read aloud with a partner.

Situation 1

A family is getting ready for bed.

爸爸：你想幾點鐘起來？　　　What time are you thinking of getting up?

媽媽：六點半或者六點　　　　Six thirty or six forty-five.
　　　三刻。你呢？　　　　　How about you?

爸爸：我六點或者六點差　　　I'll get up at six or ten to six.
　　　十分起來。

Situation 2

A woman approaches a police officer.

女的：請問，現在幾點鐘？　　May I ask what time it is?

警察：兩點過十分。　　　　　Ten past two.

Situation 3

Wang Jin hangs up the telephone and continues reading. Her brother Wang Xing comes into the room.

王星：剛才誰來電話？   Who called just now?

王今：二伯。   Second Uncle.

王星：他說甚麼了？   What did he say?

王今：他說伯母一會兒會來。   He said Aunty will come in a while.

5. Summary. For each word in English, fill in the *pinyin* , the corresponding number for traditional characters and the corresponding letter for simplified characters.

business hours	*yíngyè shíjiān*		
to (written style)	*zhì*		
9:30			
9:30 (written style)			
to have a simple meal	*chī biànfàn*		
to get up			
in a while			
at what time			
or	*huòzhě*		
6:45			
5:50			
now	*xiànzài*		
a moment ago	*gāngcái*		
to speak			

1. 起來   a. 六点差十分
2. 六點三刻   b. 营业时间
3. 或者   c. 九点半
4. 至   d. 几点钟
5. 吃便飯   e. 至
6. 現在   f. 剛才
7. 九點半   g. 现在
8. 幾點鐘   h. 六点三刻
9. 營業時間   i. 说话
10. 一會兒   j. 9时30分
11. 剛才   k. 起来
12. 六點差十分 l. 一会儿
13. 9時30分   m. 吃便饭
14. 说話   n. 或者

6. Practice writing.

7. Write any three ways of expressing each of the following.

5:30	五點半	五時三十分	5時30分
6:55			
7:10			
8:15	8時15分	八點一刻	
9:05			

8. Write a note to a friend, suggesting that you meet at 4:00. Have your friend call you to confirm the meeting; provide your telephone number.

SEGMENT B: Time by divisions of the day.

• Which of the two signs on this page appears in the PRC?

• Circle and label the word for "morning."

• Circle and label the word for "evening."

営 業 時 間

早 9:00 一 晩 5:30

2. Transcribe this sign (fill in the blanks below).

yíng _yè_ _____ _____

zhì

_____ _____ _____ _____ _____

3. "Service Hours"

• Circle and label the characters for "a.m."

• Circle and label the characters for "p.m."

4. Read aloud with a partner.

<u>Situation 1</u>

A worried family hovers over the bed of a cranky child.

爸爸：李醫生八點鐘來。   Dr. Li will be here at eight.

媽媽：早上八點鐘還是晚   Eight in the morning or
        上八點鐘？   eight in the evening?

爸爸：晚上八點。   Eight in the evening.

<u>Situation 2</u>

A teacher and student are passing the time of day.

學生：老師，您幾點鐘吃   Teacher, what time do you eat
        早飯？   breakfast?

老師：我不吃早飯。   I don't eat breakfast.

學生： 午飯呢？　　　　　　　　　　How about lunch?

老師： 差不多都是在十二點鐘　　　I almost always eat lunch at twelve.
　　　 吃午飯。你呢，小黃？　　　How about you, Xiao Huang?

學生： 我不吃午飯，我晚飯　　　　I don't eat lunch. I eat dinner very
　　　 吃得很早。　　　　　　　　early.

老師： 你夜裡不餓嗎？　　　　　　Don't you get hungry at night?

學生： 睡着了就不覺得餓了。　　　After I fall asleep I don't feel hungry.

老師： 我跟你不一樣。我要是　　　You and I aren't the same. If I eat
　　　 晚飯吃得早，半夜還得　　　dinner early, I have to get up in the
　　　 起來吃東西。　　　　　　　middle of the night to eat something.

5. Write numbers in the blanks to indicate the correct order of the sentences in each paragraph. Proceed from the earliest to the latest events.

	下午五點鐘我到朋友的家裡去。
	我們晚上去看八點鐘的電影。
	我早上七點鐘吃早餐。

	我今天在家裡吃早飯。
	夜裡十點鐘出去看朋友。
	八點在家裡吃晚飯。
	上午九點要去見老師。
	下午在家裡休息。

	我天天早上去散步。
	吃晚飯以前先洗澡。
	我中午跟我妹妹一塊兒吃飯。

6. Summary. For each word in English, fill in the *pinyin* , the corresponding number for traditional characters and the corresponding letter for simplified characters.

morning			
evening			
a.m.			
p.m.			
(X) or (Y)?			
breakfast			
lunch			
dinner			
just about, almost			
at night			
I am not the same as you.			
if			
midnight			
movie			
every day			
together			
at home			

1. 還是
2. 午/中飯
3. 晚上
4. 要是
5. 差不多
6. 早上
7. 電影
8. 下午
9. 晚餐
10. 天天
11. 上午
12. 早飯/餐
13. 夜裡
14. 在家裡
15. 一塊兒
16. 半夜
17. 我跟你不
一樣。

a. 天天
b. 晚餐
c. 差不多
d. 下午
e. 电影
f. 晚上
g. 要是
h. 早上
i   我跟你不
一样。
j   半夜
k. 上午
l   早饭/餐
m. 夜里
n. 在家里
o. 还是
p. 午/中饭
q. 一块儿

7. Practice writing.

*This is the common written form of 裡 .

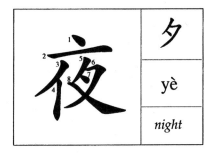

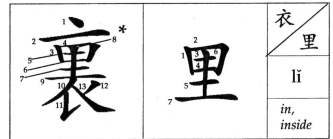

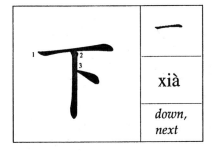

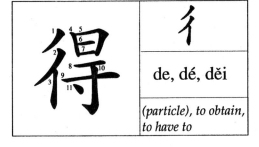

8. Rewrite this note in characters. Write from RIGHT TO LEFT.

Māma:
Zǎoshàng Xiǎohóng lái diànhuà
jiào wǒ qù tā jiā.
Wǒ xiàwǔ qù wǎnshàng
jiǔ diǎn huílái.
Wǎnshàng jiàn.

		：

來	紅			
	去		叫	

回							

9. Write a note responding to a friend who has asked to see you tomorrow morning. Since morning's not good for you, suggest the afternoon instead.

_____

_____

_____

_____

_____

_____

SEGMENT C: Time by week, month, and year.

1. On which day(s) is this store open 9–12 and 1:30–4(?)? ➡

On which day(s) is it closed?

Guess which day(s) it is open 9–12:30 and 2–5:00.

2. Rewrite this sign in English. ➡

```
_____

____ : ____   to  _____

____ : ____   to  _____

_____
```

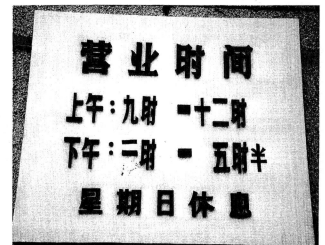

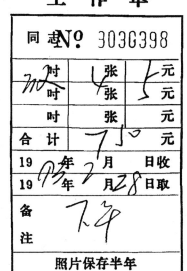

⬅ 3. This is a work order receipt from a camera-shop, specifying 4 reprints.

•The customer is to pick up the order on *February 28, 1993*, in the *afternoon.* Highlight this information on the receipt.

•On the line marked " 1," the attendant is to fill in when the order was received. (This line is blank on the receipt.) Circle and label the word "to receive."

•Line 2 indicates when the customer is to pick up the completed order. "To pick up, retrieve" is qǔ. Circle and label this word.

4. "INVITATION"

《請柬》

謹詹於國曆 81 年 11 月 10 日

星期二 下午 5 時 45 分

假座 貴賓 廳敬備菲酌

恭候

光臨

鄭鴻財謹邀

GOLDEN DOUBLE BLISS CO. LTD. SINCE 1981

金 雙 囍 大 酒 樓
台北市延平南路110號
新生報業大樓15樓(中山堂側)
總　　　機：3613181～5

港式飲茶　　　　　　粵 湘 名 菜
中式自助餐　　　　　結婚廣場700坪

Fill in the following chart with information extracted from the invitation.

* The year as indicated here follows the custom of the Republic of China (ROC, now on Taiwan), which was established in 1911. Year 1 by the ROC calendar is 1912. To convert to the Western system, add 1911 to the year stated.

year*	1992
month	
day	
day of the week	
time	

間　時　業　營

五期星至一期星（一）
分十三時三午下至時九午上
時二十至時九午上六期星（二）

息休日期星假例

5. Rewrite in English.

BUSINESS HOURS

1. _____

_____

2. _____

Closed on holidays and _____

• The word for "holiday" is lìjià. Circle and label it.

6. Read aloud with a partner.

<u>Situation 1</u>

It is break time in a law office.

秘書：張律師，您星期幾
　　　過生日？

Attorney Chang, what day
of the week is your birthday?

律師：星期六吧。跟你一
　　　樣，是不是？。

Saturday, I think. The
same as you, right?

秘書：不。我的生日是星
　　　期四。我太太星期
　　　六也過生日。

No. My birthday is Thursday.
My wife's birthday is on also on
Saturday.

<u>Situation 2</u>

A secretary stops by an attorney's office.

秘書：陳律師，您這個
　　　禮拜是不是要和李
　　　女士吃午飯？

Attorney Chen, you are
having lunch this week with
Ms. Li?

律師：是。我們禮拜天一起
　　　吃午飯。

Yes. We are having lunch on
Sunday.

秘書：爲甚麼禮拜天呢？

Why Sunday?

律師：因爲她星期一到星
　　　期六都很忙。

Because she's busy from Monday
through Saturday.

7. Summary. For each word in English, fill in the *pinyin*, the corresponding number for traditional characters and the corresponding letter for simplified characters.

week	*xīngqī*		
week			
which day of the week			
February			
to pick up, retrieve	*qǔ*		
to celebrate a birthday			
to go	*qù*		
with, and			
together	*yìqǐ*		
because			

1. 星期幾　　a. 取
2. 過生日　　b. 礼拜
3. 和　　　　c. 二月
4. 取　　　　d. 一起
5. 星期　　　e. 星期几
6. 一起　　　f. 去
7. 禮拜　　　g. 星期
8. 因爲　　　h. 和
9. 去　　　　i. 过生日
10. 二月　　　j. 因为

8. Practice writing.

星　日　xīng　star

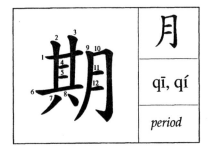

期　月　qī, qí　period

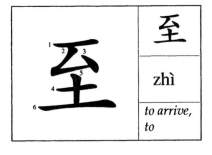

至　至　zhì　to arrive, to

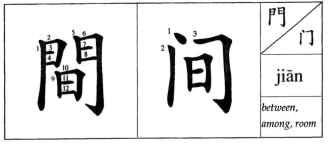

間　间　門　门　jiān　between, among, room

9. The sign below appears on the door of a shop that is usually open from 9 am to 5:30 pm, but is closed Sundays. Fill in the missing characters.

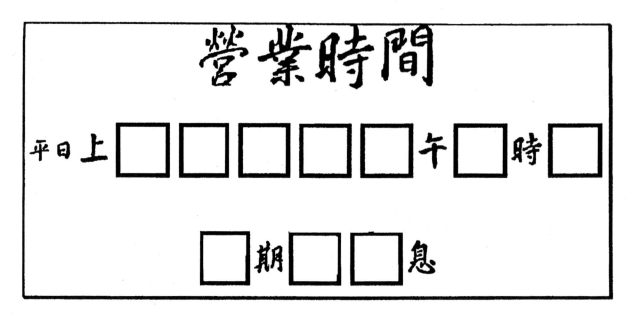

10. A friend would like to share a meal with you soon, and would like to know when you usually eat. Write a note stating when you eat your three meals every day.

SEGMENT D: Relative time by day and week.

1. Figure out the relationships and fill in the blanks in English.

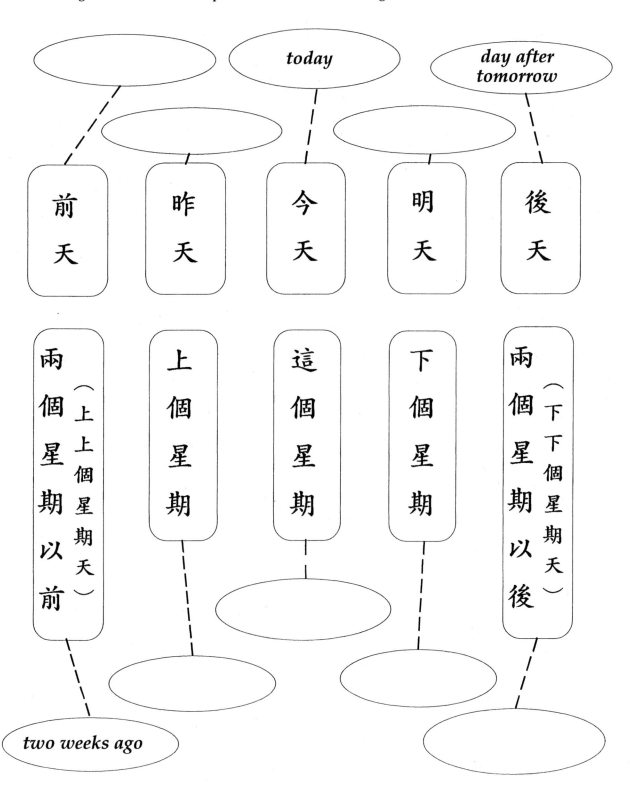

我们下星期一下午三点半
在学校图书馆见面，好吗？

2. The author of this note suggests meeting at the school library. When does she propose to meet?

Answer: _____

3. Read aloud with a partner.

Two classmates are trying to arrange a time to meet.

男生：你甚麼時候有空？　　　When are you free?

女生：今天明天都
　　　有空。　　　　　　　　Today or tomorrow would be fine.

男生：今天明天我沒
　　　空。後天呢？　　　　　I'm not free today or tomorrow. How about the day after that?

女生：後天我沒空。那就
　　　下個星期吧。　　　　　I'm not free the day after tomorrow. Next week, then?

男生：下個星期行。
　　　哪天？　　　　　　　　Next week's fine. Which day?

女生：星期二怎麼樣？　　　How is next Tuesday?

男生：行，就下個星期
　　　二吧。　　　　　　　　Fine. Let's make it next Tuesday, then.

4. Summary. For each word in English, fill in the *pinyin*, the corresponding number for traditional characters and the corresponding letter for simplified characters.

day before yesterday			
yesterday			
today			
tomorrow			
day after tomorrow			
three days from now			
four days ago			
this week			
last week			
next week			
next Sunday			
to have free time			

1. 三天以後　　a. 前天
2. 明天　　　　b. 四天以前
3. 昨天　　　　c. 这个星期
4. 後天　　　　d. 明天
5. 這個星期　　e. 下个星期天
6. 下個星期天　f. 后天
7. 今天　　　　g. 下个星期
8. 前天　　　　h. 今天
9. 上個星期　　i. 三天以后
10. 有空　　　　j. 昨天
11. 下個星期　　k. 上个星期
12. 四天以前　　l. 有空

5. Practice writing.

人 jīn

now

日 míng

bright, clear

大 tiān

sky, day

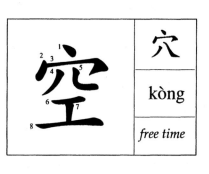

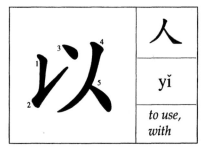

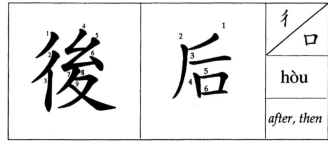

6. A friend has asked you to meet him tomorrow afternoon. Write the following response in characters.

> Duìbuqǐ. Wǒ míngtiān xiàwǔ méi kòng. Hòutiān wǎnshàng chī le wǎnfàn yǐhòu kěyǐ ma?

_____

_____

_____

Now pretend you are the friend. Respond to the note above, agreeing to meet at the time and date designated.

_____

_____

_____

SEGMENT E: Relative time by month, year and season.

1. Write *pinyin* in the empty circles.

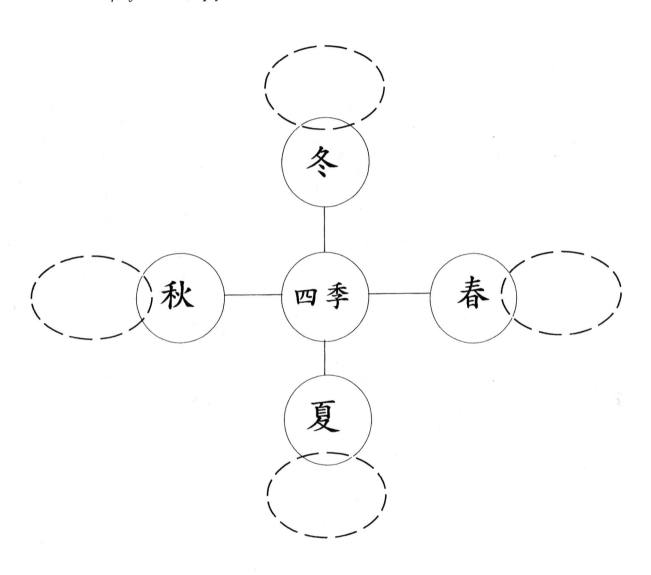

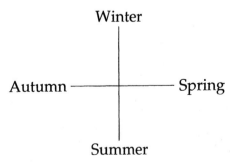

"Notice"

佈告

本校春季旅行定在四月六日上午
九時出發。參加者請八時四十五
分在圖書館前面集合。

校長
張美德
八十二年四月一日

2. This notice is like many posted on the bulletin boards of schools in Taiwan. Fill in the blanks in the English version.

The school _____ trip will depart on April _____

at _____ a.m. Participants please gather at

_____ in front of the library.

_____ , principal

_____

3. Read aloud with a partner.

Situation 1

Two teachers are chatting.

小陳： 一年四季你最喜歡哪個？   Of the four seasons in the year, which do you like best?

老張： 我最愛夏天。   I love summer the most.

小陳： 為甚麼？   Why?

老張： 夏天不上學。   There's no school in summer.

小陳： 我呢，最愛秋天。   Me, I love autumn.

老張： 為甚麼？   Why?

小陳： 秋天開學。   School starts in autumn.

Situation 2

A mother is speaking with a daughter home for the holidays.

媽媽： 你昨天做甚麼了？   What did you do yesterday?

小妹： 沒做甚麼。   I didn't do anything.

媽媽： 你今天做甚麼？   What are you doing today?

小妹： 不做甚麼。   I'm not doing anything.

媽媽： 明天呢？   How about tomorrow?

小妹： 也不做甚麼。   I won't be doing anything either.

媽媽： 明年春天呢？   How about spring next year?

小妹： 也不做甚麼。我冬天去日本。   I won't be doing anything either. I'll go to Japan in the winter.

4. Following is a moral poem told as a warning to children who put things off.

春天不是讀書天。

夏天炎炎正好眠。

待到秋來冬又至，

不如且待到明年。

Springtime is not a time to study.
In summer's heat it is best to sleep.
When autumn comes, winter is near—
we may as well dally until next year.

- Circle the terms for each of the four seasons.

- Circle the term for "next year."

- Fill in the blanks in the transliteration to the right.

_____ _____ _____ _____ dú shū tiān.

_____ _____ yán yán zhèng hǎo mián.

Dài dào _____ _____ _____ yòu _____ ,

_____ rú qiě dài dào _____ _____ .

5. Summary. For each word in English, fill in the *pinyin* , the corresponding number for traditional characters and the corresponding letter for simplified characters.

last year			
this year			
next year			
the 4 seasons			
spring			
summer			
autumn			
winter			
why			
to do, make			

1. 春天　　a. 做

2. 秋天　　b. 夏天

3. 今年　　c. 明年

4. 爲甚麼　d. 冬天

5. 去年　　e. 春天

6. 四季　　f. 为什么

7. 做　　　g. 四季

8. 夏天　　h. 去年

9. 冬天　　i. 今年

10. 明年　　j. 秋天

6. Practice writing.

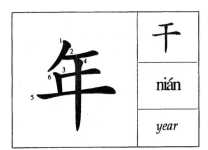

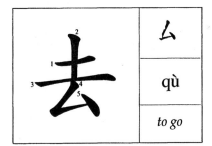

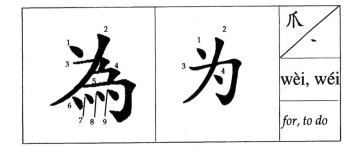

7. Your teacher has asked for information about your friend who will be arriving from China. Write him the following note in characters.

> Lǎoshī:
>
> 　　Lǐ Jǐn xià ge lǐbài xīngqīliù zǎoshàng wǔdiǎn bàn dào (arrive), xià ge yuè shíqī hào zǒu (depart). Tā qùnián liù yuè lái guò Měiguó. Míngnián xiàtiān hái lái.
>
> 　　　　　　　　　　　　　　　　Xuéshēng (your name) shàng

□□ :

□ 今 □ □ □ □ □ □ □

□ 到 ， □ □ □ □ 走 。 □

□ □ □ 過 □ □ 。 □ □ 還 □ 。

　　　　　　□ □ □ □ □

8. You receive the following note from your best friend (who has read the notice about the spring trip in this lesson).

春季旅行我不去。你去嗎？

Respond to the note. Ask why s/he's not going. Say that you want to go.

SEGMENT A: Basic monetary transactions.

1. This is a receipt from a store in the Beijing Hotel.

• How many items were purchased? _____

• What was the date of the purchase? _____

• What was the cost of the item? _____

• The term for invoice is fāpiào. Circle and label these two characters.

2. Look at the seven right-most columns. How are they labeled, and how do these labels indicate the purchase price?

• Label each column with *pinyin* selected from the list below.

bǎi yuán wàn
fēn qiān shí
jiǎo

北京 **B** 饭店
BEIJING HOTEL
台照
To

商品部销货专用发票
Shopping Service-Sales Invoice

19_90_ 年 月 日   商字№ 0013703

甲自发

编 号 Number	品 名 Name of Goods	数量 Quantity	单位 Unit	单 价 Unit Price	万	千	百	十	元	角	分
	人字	1	4	70				7	0	0	
大 写 Total Amount (capital)								7	0	0	

制 单 人
Clerk

二、交宾客

3. This is the front and back of a rénmínbì (RMB—People's currency), the currency of the PRC.

• Which of the following denominations is this note?

¥1.00 ☐
¥.10 ☐
¥.01 ☐

• Circle the characters and the *pinyin* for "People's Bank of China" (China People's Bank).

• Insert the tones above the *pinyin* words on the reverse of the note.

4. Label each note with a selection from the list.
> a. ¥5.00
> b. ¥2.00
> c. ¥.50
> d. ¥.10
> e. ¥.01

5. Label each banknote on the facing page with its place of origin: the PRC, the Republic of China on Taiwan, and Hong Kong.

Circle and label the words Zhōnghuá Mínguó (Republic of China).

Circle and label the words Xiānggǎng (Hong Kong).

6. Refer back to the banknotes and note the <u>capital</u> forms of Chinese numerals. These are used to guard against tampering, much the same way a bank check in English might read "One hundred and ten dollars only" rather than "$110." Match the capital numbers in the circles to the numbers at the bottom of the page.

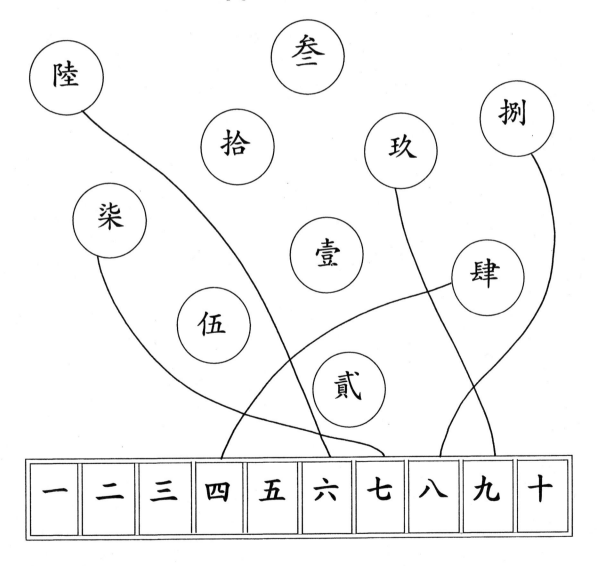

7. This is a receipt from the South Taipei branch of the International Commercial Bank of China, for an exchange of Taiwan currency for US dollars.

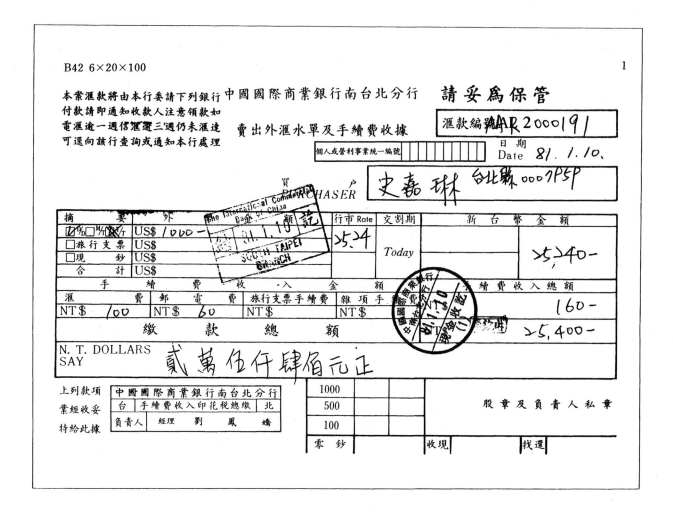

• Circle the Chinese characters for the name of the bank.

• The total amount in Taiwan currency (NT$ for "New Taiwan dollars") was NT$25,400. Circle the capital character version of this amount.

• Label each capital numeral in the amount in *pinyin*. Capital numerals are pronounced exactly the same as regular numerals.

• The last two characters in the amount are yuán (dollars) and zhèng (exactly). Circle and label these.

a.　　　　　　　　b.

c.

8. These are ticket stubs, a. and b. from a public city bus, and c. from a long-distance public bus. How much was paid for each ticket?

a. _____   b. _____   c. _____

9. This sign marks a pay _____.

To enter, each person pays　　　▢ ¥3.00　　　▢ ¥.30　　　▢ ¥.03

Shōufèi means "(we) collect/receive a fee." Circle and label these two characters.

"Each person" is měi rén, which is a shortened form of měi ge rén. Circle and label these two characters.

10. "Ticket Price."

• What is the normal ticket price per person? Answer: _____

• The sign also states, "Children under _____ are free." (Fill in the blank.)

• Piàojià means ticket price. Circle and label these two characters.

• Gài bú tuì piào means "(We will) absolutely not refund your ticket." Gài means "categorically, without exception." Write the English equivalent of each of the other characters.

bù _____   tuì _____   piào _____

• At what time will the ticket office close? Answer: _____

11. Read the amounts on the "receipt" below and write the equivalents in the space provided.

万	千	百	十	元	角	分	
	2	8	8	0			¥2,880.00
7	5	2	9	8			_____
		5	0	6	4	6	¥506.46
				7	4	0	_____
					9	0	_____

12. Pretend you are a Chinese salesclerk. Fill out the "receipt" below based on the various "pricetags" below right.

万	千	百	十	元	角	分
			8	5	0	0
1	2	2	5	0		

捌拾伍圓

¥3.50

79元

伍圓

¥1,2250

拾元

| 5元　8角　　分 |
| 元　6角　　分 |
| 元　　角　4分 |

13. Read aloud with a partner.

Li is shopping at the stall of a roadside vendor.

老李：這個多少錢？　　How much is this?

店員：九十九塊九毛九。　99 *yuan* and 99 *fen*.

老李：太貴了！便宜
　　　點兒吧！　　That's too much! Make it cheaper, okay?

店員：九十五塊好嗎？　Is 95 *yuan* alright?

老李：七十塊怎麼樣？　How about 70 *yuan*?

店員：那八十塊吧。
　　　不能再便宜了。　80 then. It can't be any cheaper than that.

老李：好吧。八十塊。　Alright then. 80 *yuan*.

14. Summary. For each word in English, fill in the *pinyin*, the corresponding number for traditional characters and the corresponding letter for simplified characters.

invoice			
price			
10,000			
1,000			
100			
¥1			
¥.10			
¥.01			
pay toilet			
each (person)			
how much?			
expensive			
inexpensive			

1. 一圓　　　　a. 一千

2. 收費廁所　b. 一百

3. 一千　　　　c. 一角

4. 多少錢？　d. 一分

5. 發票　　　　e. 貴

6. 一分　　　　f. 一万

7. 一百　　　　g. 发票

8. 便宜　　　　h. 一圓

9. 每人　　　　i. 多少钱？

10. 價錢　　　j. 收费厕所

11. 一角　　　k. 便宜

12. 貴　　　　l. 每人

13. 一萬　　　m. 价钱

15. Practice writing.

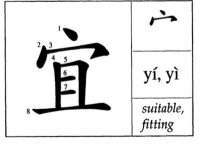

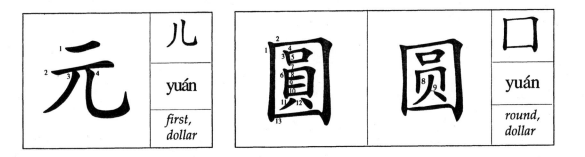

16. You find this note from someone you've asked to shop for a jacket for you.

> 559圓的好嗎？

Respond. Say that ¥559 is too expensive. Ask if there are any for ¥400. (Yǒu 400 yuán de ma?)

17. Look at the prices in column 1.

•Write out the amount in characters, using written (literary) style in column 2 and spoken (colloquial) style in column 3.

•Pretend that your standard is that ¥5 and below is inexpensive, and everything else is expensive. In column 4, rate each price 很貴，有一點貴，便宜，or 很便宜.

1. 價錢	2. Written style 書面語	3. Spoken style 口語	4. Rating
¥5	五元	五塊錢	便宜
¥3.95			
¥10.25			
¥7.70			
¥.05			
¥106			

SEGMENT B: Color, size and shape.

1. Write *pinyin* in the blank spaces provided.

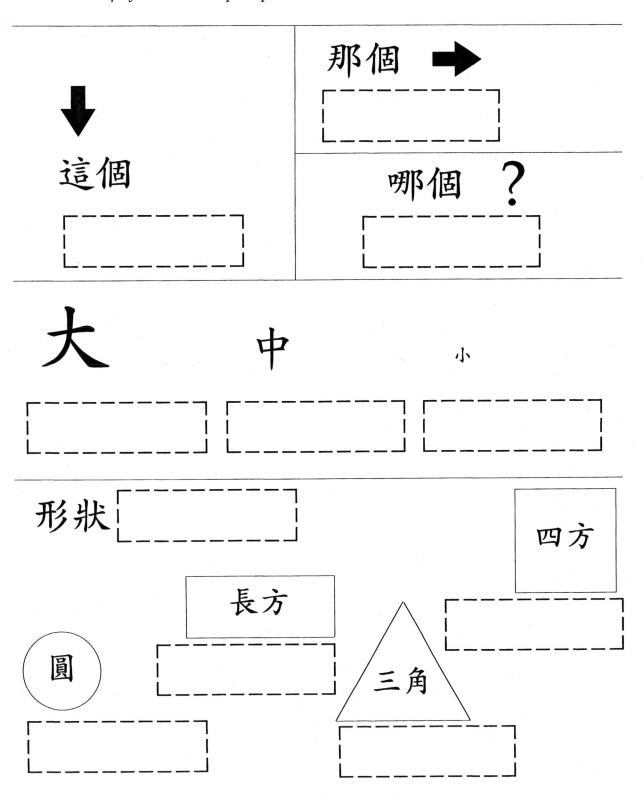

2. This is a page from the <u>Xīnhuá</u> dictionary, a popular pocket character dictionary from the Commercial Press, Beijing.

xǐng-xǐng 475

南省。
㊁ yíng 见 511 页。

刑 xíng ㄒㄧㄥˊ ❶刑罚，对犯人各种处罚的总称：死~. 徒~. 缓~. ❷反动统治阶级的刑法(fǎ)，如拷打、折磨等：受~. 动~.

型 xíng ㄒㄧㄥˊ ❶铸造器物用的模子。❷样式：小~汽车. 新~.

形 xíng ㄒㄧㄥˊ ❶样子：三角~. 地~. ~式. 创造~象. [形成]逐渐发展成为某种事物：爱护公物已~~一种风气. [形势]1.地理上指地势的高低，山、水的样子. 2.事物发展的状况：国际~~. ❷体，实体：~影不离. ❸表现：喜怒不~于色. [形容]1.面容：~~枯槁. 2. 对事物的样子、性质加以描述. [形容词]表示事物的特征、性质、状态的词，如大、小、好、坏等. ❹对照，比较：相~之下. 相~见绌.

邢 xíng ㄒㄧㄥˊ 姓.

铏 xíng ㄒㄧㄥˊ 古代盛酒器。又用于人名。

硎 xíng ㄒㄧㄥˊ 磨刀石。

铏 xíng ㄒㄧㄥˊ 古代盛羹的器具。

陉(陘) xíng ㄒㄧㄥˊ 山脉中断的地方。

饧(餳) xíng ㄒㄧㄥˊ ❶糖稀。❷糖块、面剂子等变软：糖~了. ❸精神不振，眼睛半睁半闭：眼睛发~.

行 ㊀ xíng ㄒㄧㄥˊ ❶走：日~千里. 步~. ㊃出外时用的：~装. ~篋. [行头](-tou)演戏时穿戴的衣物. [行李](-li)出外时所带的包裹箱子等. ❷流通，传递：~文. ~销. 通~全国. 发~报刊、书籍. 风~一时. ❸实际地做：~礼. 举~. 实~. 便宜~事. ❹(旧读 xìng)足以表明品质的举止行动：言~. 品~. 罪~. ❺可以：没准备就开会可不~. ~了，车修好了. ❻能干：你真~. ❼将要：~将毕业.
㊁ háng 见 158 页。

擤(揂) xǐng ㄒㄧㄥˇ 捏住鼻子，用气排出鼻涕：~鼻涕.

省 ㊀ xǐng ㄒㄧㄥˇ ❶检查自己：反~. ❷知觉：不~人事. ❸省悟，觉悟：猛~前非. ❹看望父母，尊亲：~亲.
㊁ shěng 见 389 页。

• What is the first meaning of the character in the marked entry?

• Circle and label the word for "triangle."

• How are entries organized in this dictionary?

3. The following is a teenager's diary entry, containing a description of a monster in a horror film. Read what you can of it, using your background knowledge of Chinese characters (especially radicals) to guess the meaning of words you don't know. Extract three facts about the monster's physical appearance and write them (in English) in the blanks provided.

一月二十九日，星期五。晴間多雲。

昨天晚上看的電影可怕極了，那個惡鬼的樣子把我嚇得夠嗆。三角形的大耳朵，紅紅的小眼睛，圓圓的大嘴巴，血淋淋的大牙齒…使我做了一夜的惡夢。

4. Read aloud with a partner.

Situation 1

Two friends are talking about some carvings in an antique shop.

王：小張，你買了哪個？　　　　Xiao Zhang, which did you buy?

張：我買了圓的。　　　　　　　I bought the round one.

王：哪個圓的？　　　　　　　　Which round one?

張：大的那個。你買了哪個？　　The big one. Which did you buy?

王：我買了一個長方的。　　　　I bought a rectangular one.

Situation 2

Li Ming is shopping for a tablecloth.

李明：我看看那個。　　　　　　I want that one.

店員：哪個？　　　　　　　　　Which one?

李明：那個四方的。　　　　　　That square one.

店員：行。　　　　　　　　　　Okay.

李明：你們賣圓的嗎？　　　　　Do you sell round ones?

店員：對不起，不賣。　　　　　Sorry, we don't.

5. Summary. For each word in English, fill in the *pinyin*, the corresponding number for traditional characters and the corresponding letter for simplified characters.

English	pinyin		
this			
that			
which			
small			
medium			
large			
size	dàxiǎo		
shape	xíngzhuàng		
circle	yuánxíng		
square			
rectangle			
triangle			
to buy			
to sell			
to be okay	xíng		

1. 買
2. 四方形
3. 哪個
4. 大
5. 三角形
6. 這個
7. 圓形
8. 中
9. 行
10. 大小
11. 賣
12. 那個
13. 長方形
14. 小
15. 形狀

a. 大
b. 卖
c. 中
d. 长方形
e. 小
f. 形状
g. 三角形
h. 行
i. 这个
j. 买
k. 哪个
l. 圆形
m. 四方形
n. 那个
o. 大小

6. Practice writing.

7. You've asked a friend to bring you a box from the store. He returns from the store while you are out, and leaves you this note.

店裡賣大的，小的，圓的，
方的。你要甚麼樣的？

Write back. Say you want a small square one that is not too expensive.

SEGMENT C: Common objects.

1. This is an advertisement for garbage bags (lājīdài in the PRC and lèsèdài in Taiwan).

What is the sale price?

The original price?

Which sizes are available?

●妙潔垃圾袋··········
大、中、小　原價18元　**15**元

Circle and label the words for "bag" and "original price."

2. Read aloud with a partner.

Situation 1

A young boy nick-named Ah Mao is shopping with his parents.

阿毛：我要買一個玩具。

I want to buy a toy.

媽媽：不行。沒有錢買玩具。

No. We don't have money
to buy toys.

Situation 2

Ah Mao has wrangled a toy from his father but is tired of carrying it.

阿毛：爸爸，你的袋子呢？

Daddy, where's your bag?

爸爸：我沒有袋子。

I don't have a bag.

Situation 3

Ah Mao has finished a bottle of juice while trying to keep up with his parents.

阿毛：媽媽，瓶子呢？

Mom, what about the bottle?

媽媽：給我吧。

Give it to me.

Situation 4

Back at home, Ah Mao is watching his older brother get ready to leave.

哥哥：我去買幾樣東西。　　　　I'm going to buy a few things.

阿毛：甚麼東西？　　　　　　　What things?

哥哥：一朵花，一份報紙，　　　A flower, a newspaper, a box of candy,
　　　一盒糖，一張畫兒。　　　and a picture.

阿毛：哦？是給誰買的？　　　　Oh? Who are you buying them for?

哥哥：不關(guān)你的事(shì)！　None of your business!

3. A woman comes home and finds the following note from her daughter Hóng'er on the table, next to a package.

媽媽：
　　　您要我去買的東西，我有一些買到了，
可是有一些沒買到，瓶子跟袋子店裏頭都了賣，
弟弟要的玩具太貴了，我沒買，盒子他們有，可是
太小了，所以也沒買，花我買了三朵，今天晚上
想送給英英。你要的糖我買了三斤，就在
桌子上。

　　　　　　　　　　　　　　　　紅兒．

Based on Hóng'er's note, the mother knows which of the items on the shopping list she gave her daughter have been purchased. Check off the items Hóng'er has <u>bought</u>.

	bag
	hard candy
	flowers for Yingying
	box to store stuffed animals
	2 bottles for birdseed
	toy for a little boy

4. Summary. For each word in English, fill in the *pinyin* , the corresponding number for traditional characters and the corresponding letter for simplified characters.

original price	*yuánjià*		
garbage bag	*lājīdài/lèsèdài*		
that book			
that bottle			
this bag			
this box			
a bottle of water			
a bag of toys			
a box of things			
a box of candy			
to give	*gěi*		
to buy X for Y			
a newspaper			
a flower			
a painting			
some things	*yì xiē dōngxi*		

1. 那個瓶子
2. 一盒東西
3. 一瓶水
4. 給 Y 買 X
5. 垃圾袋
6. 一張畫兒
7. 這個盒子
8. 給
9. 一份報紙
10. 原價
11. 一袋玩具
12. 那本書
13. 這個袋子
14. 一些東西
15. 一盒糖
16. 一朵花

a. 原价
b. 这个袋子
c. 给
d. 那本书
e. 这个盒子
f. 一袋玩具
g. 一些东西
h. 一盒糖
i. 垃圾袋
j. 一张画儿
k. 一份报纸
l. 一瓶水
m. 那个瓶子
n. 一朵花
o. 一盒东西
p. 给 Y 买 X

5. Practice writing.

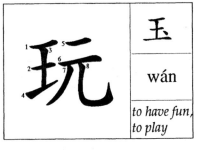

玉
wán

to have fun, to play

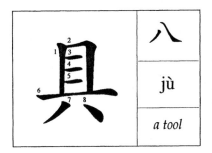

八
jù

a tool

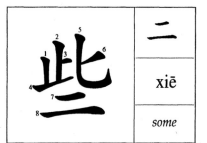

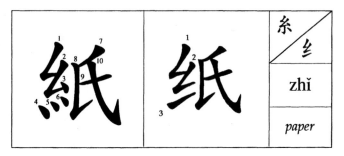

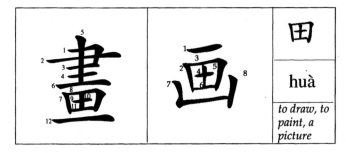

6. You are the second child in your family. You come home and see this note: ➡

老二：

去買一份晚報。

　　　　　媽

You however have to rush out and won't be home the rest of the evening. Write a note to your younger brother asking him to do the chore. Have him pick up another item (specify what) for you as well.

老三：

_____

_____

_____

SEGMENT D: Clothing

1. A teenage girl is taking stock of her best friend's wardrobe, and has produced a list in Chinese characters.

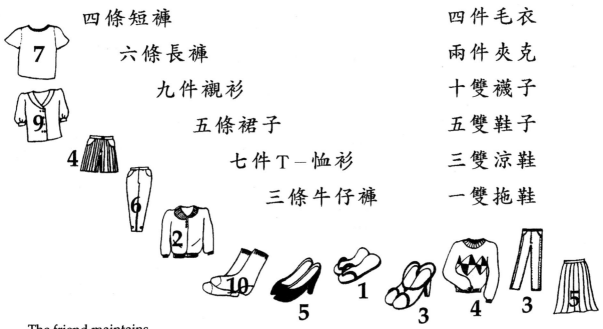

四條短褲　　　　　　四件毛衣

六條長褲　　　　　　兩件夾克

九件襯衫　　　　　　十雙襪子

五條裙子　　　　　　五雙鞋子

七件 T－恤衫　　　　三雙涼鞋

三條牛仔褲　　　　　一雙拖鞋

The friend maintains her own inventory, using Arabic numerals and pictures. Draw lines matching each item on the girl's list with the corresponding item on her friend's list.

2. Read aloud with a partner.

Situation 1

A man sees his son about to leave the house.

爸爸：你穿這件衣服不合適。　　The clothes you're wearing are not suitable.

小弟：怎麼不合適？　　　　　　How so?

爸爸：太黑了。　　　　　　　　They are too dark.

Situation 2

Lao Huang is shopping for shoes.

店員：這雙鞋子怎麼樣？　　　　How is this pair of shoes?

老黃：很好，很合適。　　　　　Fine, they fit well.

3. Match the captions to the photographs.

<blockquote>

小女孩兒穿一件連衣裙，一雙長筒襪子。

有兩個女的，一個穿襯衫和短褲，一個穿襯衫和長褲。

有一個老頭兒，只穿短褲，不穿別的。

</blockquote>

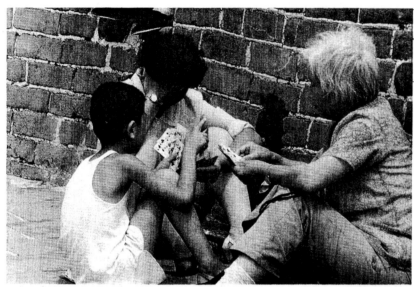

a

b | c

•A "dress" is a "liányīqún." Circle and label this term.

•"Lǎotóur" means "old fellow." Circle and label this term.

•Circle and label two occurences of the word "hé" meaning "and."

4. Summary. For each word in English, fill in the *pinyin*, the corresponding number for traditional characters and the corresponding letter for simplified characters.

to wear			
general measure word for clothes	*jiàn*		
clothes			
a pair			
fitting, suitable			
dress	*liányīqún*		
shirt			
trousers, pants			
shorts			
sweater			
jacket			
shoes			
and	*hé*		
old fellow, old man			

1. 件　　　　　a. 毛衣
2. 褲子　　　　b. 老头儿
3. 鞋子　　　　c. 穿
4. 連衣裙　　　d. 夹克
5. 毛衣　　　　e. 合适
6. 穿　　　　　f. 短裤
7. 一雙　　　　g. 衣服
8. 和　　　　　h. 衬衫
9. 短褲　　　　i. 鞋子
10. 老頭兒　　　j. 件
11. 衣服　　　　k. 一双
12. 襯衫　　　　l. 和
13. 夾克　　　　m. 连衣裙
14. 合適　　　　n. 裤子

5. Practice writing.

件　人
jiàn
item, (measure word)

衣
yī
clothing

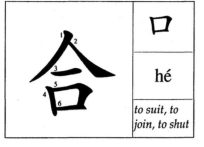

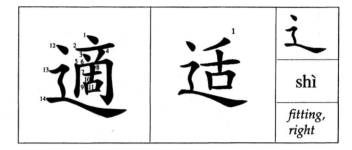

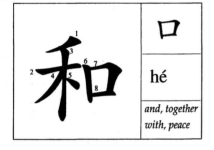

老二：

我給你們買了幾件衣服。不知你

穿合適不合適。你穿多大號？

三姨

6. Your third aunt comes to town with a suitcase full of clothing (purchased at very low prices in Hong Kong) and sends you this note.

三姨：

_____

_____

_____

_____

_____

Respond briefly and courteously.

SEGMENT E: Comparing size, color, price and quantity.

1. Write the *pinyin* for each character below.

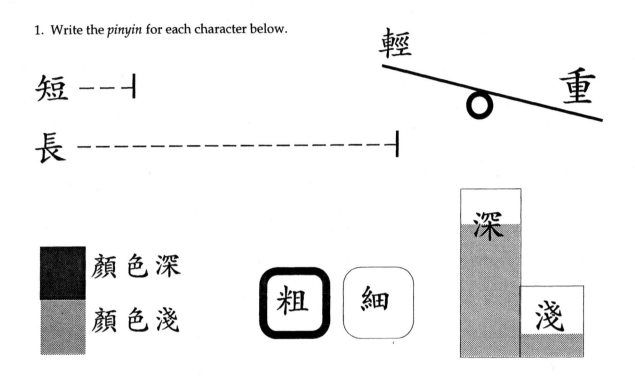

2. Read aloud with a partner.

<u>Situation 1</u>

A man speaks to his wife as he leaves the house.

父親： 我去給小紅買個書包。   I'm going to buy a book bag for Xiao Hong.

母親： 甚麼樣的書包？   What kind of book bag?

父親： 一個大點的，輕點的。   A large, light one.

<u>Situation 2</u>

A woman is shopping for skirts.

店員： 你要長的要短的？   Do you want a long or short one?

小姐： 我要長的。   I want a long one.

Situation 3

Two students are looking at marking pens in a stationery store.

王：　這樣的太粗了。沒有細一
　　　點兒的嗎？

This kind is too thick. Aren't there any finer ones?

白：　有。這樣的可以嗎？

There are. Will this type do?

Situation 4

A woman is shopping with her husband.

太太：你覺得這件衣服怎麼樣？

What do you think of this (item of clothing)?

先生：顏色太淺了一點兒。

The color is a little too light.

太太：不，我喜歡顏色淺的。顏
　　　色深的不好看。

No it isn't. I like light-colored things. Dark things don't look good.

3. You are the clerk in a sundry store. The notes on the left were written by customers and pinned to items for sale. The notes on the right were written in response by your manager as instructions to you, but got mixed up. Match the notes on the right to those on the left. (Zhǎo 找 = to find; méi bànfǎ 沒辦法 = "It can't be helped")

太粗了。

有輕點兒的嗎？
問問小李。

太小了。

這條褲子
太長了。

粗的好！細的也
有。找一個給他。

盒子太重了。

找一件大的。

沒辦法。沒
有深色的。

這幾件衣服顏
色都太淺。

去找一條短一
點兒的給他。

4. Summary. For each word in English, fill in the *pinyin*, the corresponding number for traditional characters and the corresponding letter for simplified characters.

light			
heavy			
long			
short			
coarse			
fine			
deep			
shallow			
dark in color			
light in color			
this kind			
these few things			
good enough	*gòu hǎo*		

1. 深   a. 重
2. 重   b. 粗
3. 這樣的   c. 細
4. 顏色深   d. 这样的
5. 長   e. 轻
6. 細   f. 深
7. 顏色淺   g. 长
8. 輕   h. 这几样东西
9. 粗   i. 浅
10. 這幾樣東西   j. 颜色浅
11. 淺   k. 短
12. 短   l. 够好
13. 夠好   m. 颜色深

5. Practice writing.

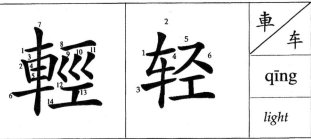

短	矢 duǎn short

長	长	長 ╱ ノ cháng long

夠	够	夕 gòu enough

6. You have returned from a shopping trip taken on behalf of some demanding and ungrateful friends, who send you the following notes. Respond to each (politely). ➡

給	给	糸 gěi to give, for

_____

盒子太重了。店裡沒有輕的嗎？

_____

你給我買的鞋子太大了。

_____

那条裤子不够长！怎么办？

SEGMENT A: Preferences in colors

1. Write the *pinyin* for the characters. Then color each segment in the circle to match its label.

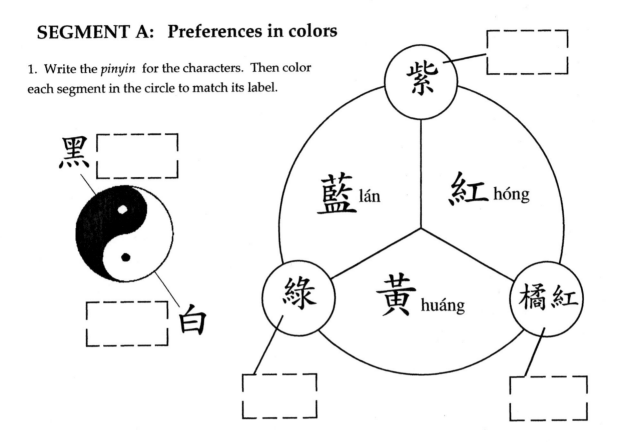

2. This is a portion of a physical examination report form from a Taipei hospital.

一. 檢查結果

健康檢查 項　目	醫　師　檢　查　結　果
1.辨　色　力	☐正常　☐紅　☐綠　☐黃　☐藍色 ☐盲　☐弱
2.　　眼	☐無特殊發現 斜視：☐右　☐左　☐交替　☐內　☐外 　　　☐垂直　☐間歇　☐斜位　☐眼瞼下 　　垂　☐睫毛倒插　☐眼球振顫 眼瞼部傷痕：☐面　☐瞼　☐眼球　☐G 　　　　　☐P　☐F　☐C

◄ Item #1 is color perception.

Fill in the blanks in the English equivalent of this item. ↓

"Blind" is máng. What is "weak?"

Answer: _____

☐ normal　☐____　☐____　☐____　☐____

☐ blind　☐ weak

3. Fill in the blanks below with selections from the list provided.

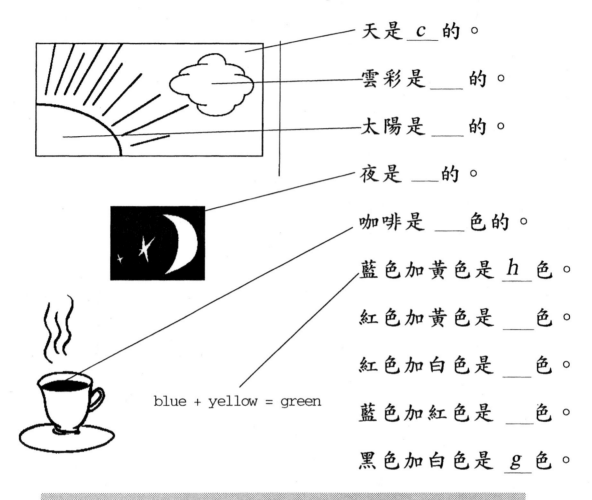

天是 _c_ 的。

雲彩是 ___ 的。

太陽是 ___ 的。

夜是 ___ 的。

咖啡是 ___ 色的。

藍色加黃色是 _h_ 色。

紅色加黃色是 ___ 色。

紅色加白色是 ___ 色。

藍色加紅色是 ___ 色。

黑色加白色是 _g_ 色。

blue + yellow = green

a.黑　b.紫　c.藍　d.咖啡　e.白　f.粉紅　g.灰　h.綠　i.黃　j.橘紅

4. Read the note on the next page, and, following the key provided, fill in the blanks below.

Amount	Item	Color
3	erasers	white
	balloons	
	apples	
	pens	
	hats	

王則甚：

你好！你答應我進城時幫我買些東西，真謝々你。我要的東西都寫在下面了：

—— 兩支黑筆
—— 三塊白橡皮
—— 十二隻綠氣球
—— 一頂藍帽子
—— 四個紅蘋果

KEY:

 蘋果 氣球  橡皮 帽子 筆

5. Read aloud with a partner.

<u>Situation 1</u>

Two 14-year olds are sitting beneath a tree.

大中：你喜歡我嗎？	Do you like me?
小美：我不說。	I'm not going to say.
大中：你討厭我嗎？	Do you hate me?
小美：也不說。你愛我嗎？	I'm not going to say that either. Do you love me?
大中：我…我不愛你。	I...I don't love you.

Situation 2

Li is hosting two visitors at a reception.

李： 馬先生，您喝咖啡嗎？   Mr. Ma, will you drink coffee?

馬： 不，我喝茶，謝謝。   No, I'll have tea, thank you.

李： 白小姐呢？   How about you, Miss Bai?

白： 我喝咖啡。   I'll have coffee.

Situation 3

Chen is shopping for a photo-album.

店員： 您要金色的嗎？   Would you like a gold one?

老陳： 有銀色的嗎？   Is there a silver one?

店員： 對不起，沒有。   Sorry, no.

老陳： 藍色的呢？   How about a blue one?

店員： 有…這是藍色的。   Yes...this is blue.

老陳： 不…那是綠色的。   No...that's green.

店員： 哦，對…是綠的。對不起，我們沒有藍的。紅的、黃的怎麼樣？   Oh, right...it's green. Sorry, we don't have a blue one. How about red or yellow?

老陳： 沒有粉紅的嗎？   Isn't there any pink?

店員： 沒有。   No there isn't.

老陳： 你們有甚麼顏色呢？   What colors do you have?

店員： 有金的、綠的、紅的、黃的、和…沒有了。   We have gold, green, red, yellow, and...that's all.

老陳： 那些顏色我都不怎麼喜歡。不過…謝謝了。   I don't like any of those colors very much. Well, thank you anyway.

6. Summary. For each word in English, fill in the *pinyin*, the corresponding number for traditional characters and the corresponding letter for simplified characters.

English	pinyin		
color			
blue			
red			
yellow			
green			
purple			
orange			
pink			
brown			
black			
white			
gold			
silver			
blind (literary)			
weak			
sky	tiān		
cloud	yúncai		
sun	tàiyáng		
night	yè		
plus, to add	jiā		
apple	píngguǒ		
balloon	qìqiú		
pen	bǐ		
eraser	xiàngpí		
hat	màozi		
to like			
to love			
to hate			

1. 銀	a. 顔色
2. 蘋果	b. 蓝
3. 橘紅	c. 喜欢
4. 弱	d. 橡皮
5. 藍	e. 橘红
6. 夜	f. 咖啡色
7. 金	g. 讨厌
8. 黃	h. 紫
9. 雲彩	i. 加
10. 紫	j. 红
11. 喜歡	k. 爱
12. 咖啡色	l. 银
13. 盲	m. 白
14. 橡皮	n. 粉红
15. 黑	o. 黄
16. 討厭	p. 绿
17. 天	q. 夜
18. 顔色	r. 帽子
19. 氣球	s. 盲
20. 白	t. 苹果
21. 加	u. 笔
22. 太陽	v. 气球
23. 紅	w. 云彩
24. 綠	x. 太阳
25. 筆	y. 金
26. 粉紅	z. 天
27. 愛	aa. 黑
28. 帽子	ab. 弱

7. Practice writing.

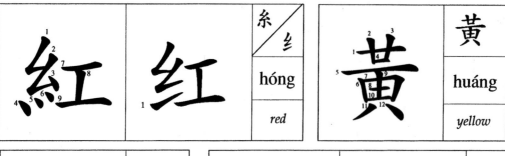

你给我买的黄衬衫和金衬衫
真好看。是在哪儿买的？店
里还有其他颜色吗？

8. You receive this note
◀ from a friend.

其他　qítā means "other."

Write a note back. Say
you bought the shirt at
遠東服裝店，and
name at least two other
color combinations
available.

SEGMENT B: Preferences in pastimes

1. Both these signs appear in the PRC. Discuss the differences between them.

What does this sign say? ➡ ➡ ➡

English: _____

pinyin: _____

⬆ "Dàibàn chángtú" means "We will dial long-distance calls for you." Circle these four characters.

2. This sign appears in Taiwan. ➡

Circle the characters "kǎshì"; guess what they mean. Hints:
- "kǎ" is a transliteration of an English word;
- "shì" means "style, type";
- these phones are not coin-operated.

3. Read aloud with a partner.

<u>Situation 1</u>

Two friends are chatting.

美英：你最喜歡做甚麼？　　　　　　　What do you most like to do?

覺心：我喜歡打電話。你呢？　　　　　I most like talking on the telephone. And you?

美英：我不喜歡打電話。　　　　　　　I don't like talking on the telephone.
　　　　我愛寫信。　　　　　　　　　I like to write letters.

<u>Situation 2</u>

A mother looks worriedly at her son.

媽媽：小弟，你在做甚麼？　　　　　　Little brother, what are you doing?

弟弟：我在看電視。　　　　　　　　　I'm watching television.

媽媽：不要看電視了。　　　　　　　　Don't watch TV anymore. Come
　　　　你來看書吧。　　　　　　　　over and do some reading.

弟弟：我一會兒來。　　　　　　　　　I'll come in a while.

<u>Situation 3</u>

Two students are talking with their language teacher.

老師：你們聽錄音了嗎？　　　　　　　Did you listen to the tapes?

女生：聽了，老師。　　　　　　　　　I did, Teacher.

男生：我也聽了。我跟她　　　　　　　I did too. I listened to them with
　　　　一塊兒聽的。　　　　　　　　her.

<u>Situation 4</u>

Two classmates meet at the park.

大中：你會打球嗎？　　　　　　　　　Can you play ball?

信一：甚麼球？　　　　　　　　　　　What kind of ball?

大中：美式足球。　　　　　　　　　　American football.

信一：會。我們一塊兒打吧。　　　　　I can. Let's play together.

Situation 5

A mother and father are discussing their absent children.

爸爸： 小弟小妹他們看
　　　電影兒去了嗎？

Did the children (little brother and little sister) go to the movies?

媽媽： 沒有，游泳去了。

No, they went swimming.

4. Read the brief statements below, then complete the task assigned.

Saturday Morning Family Snapshot

我要去看電影。

爸爸在看電視。

弟弟想寫信，可是太累了。

妹妹在打球。

媽媽在看書。

沒有人在打電話。

哥哥得聽錄音，可是他不聽。

姐姐想游泳，可是她不會。

Which of the following activities are <u>taking place</u> this Saturday morning?

	yes	no
playing ball		
reading		
listening to a tape		
talking on the phone		
swimming		
watching television		
watching a movie		
writing a letter		

5. "LET'S GO SHOPPING IN CHINATOWN"

•Highlight the characters "qù Tángrénjiē mǎi cài" (go shopping for food in Chinatown).

•Who are the two people who have already decided to go? Circle their names and label these #1 and #2.

•If Chris wants to go along, what is s/he to do? Highlight the characters that give you the answer.

Chris:

　　明天早上我和王方去唐
人街买菜，你有没有兴趣走
一趟？有的话，给我或王方
来个电话。

　　　　　　　　敏敏

6. Summary. For each word in English, fill in the *pinyin*, the corresponding number for traditional characters and the corresponding letter for simplified characters.

English	pinyin	#	letter
public telephone			
card-operated phone	*kǎshì gōngyòng diànhuà*		
What are you doing?			
watch television			
read a book			
talk on the phone			
listen to tapes			
play ball			
watch a movie			
swim			
together	*yíkuàir*		
write a letter			
buy groceries	*mǎi cài*		
but, however	*kěshì*		

1. 買菜　　　　　　a. 听录音
2. 看書　　　　　　b. 你在做什么？
3. 寫信　　　　　　c. 打电话
4. 公用電話　　　　d. 看电视
5. 打球　　　　　　e. 看电影
6. 一塊兒　　　　　f. 可是
7. 打電話　　　　　g. 游泳
8. 你在做甚麼？　　h. 卡式公用电话
9. 看電影　　　　　i. 买菜
10. 卡式公用電話　　j. 一块儿
11. 聽錄音　　　　　k. 打球
12. 可是　　　　　　l. 看书
13. 看電視　　　　　m. 公用电话
14. 游泳　　　　　　n. 写信

7. Practice writing.

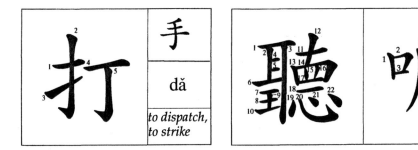

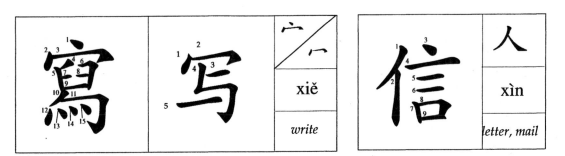

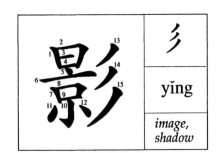

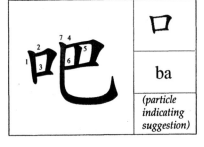

8. A PRC penfriend's letter to you includes the following statements and questions. Please respond to them.

你很长时间没给我写信了。你现在怎么样？

我最爱看电影，可是我又没钱，又没时间，所以我不常去看。你呢？

我和我妹妹天天去游泳。有时候也喜欢打打球。你呢？你爱玩什么？

1. In English, if an unfamiliar word is used in speech, the listener might ask, "How do you spell that?" to gain a clue to its identity. To identify a Chinese character, the person who used the word might use a finger to trace the character on the palm of the hand to "show" the other person. She might also break the character down into its component parts and identify it that way. Match the descriptions on the left with the characters on the right, to see how characters might be identified in speech.

"A *single standing person* on the left and a *mountain* on the right."

"A *sun* on the left and a *moon* on the right."

"A *three-dot water* on the left and a *tree* on the right."

"An *earth* on the left and the character y<u>ě</u> *(also)* on the right."

"The character *fire* on the left and the character *few* on the right."

"Three *trees*."

"A *two-dot water* on the left and the character *water* on the right."

"A *lift hand* on the left and a *mouth* on the right."

"The character h<u>é</u> of h<u>éshì</u> *(appropriate)* on top and a *hand* on the bottom."

"The character meaning *you* on top and a *heart* on the the bottom."

明
地
炒
仙
冰
扣
沐
您
森
拿

2. Match the characters below with their English equivalents, and practice writing them.

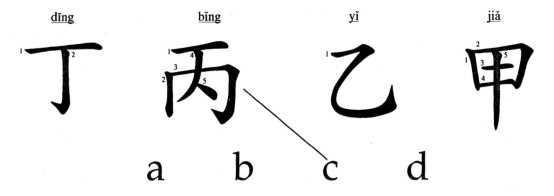

dīng   bǐng   yǐ   jiǎ

丁   丙   乙   甲

a   b   c   d

3. The characters below can be organized into four clusters based on shared PHONETIC (indicating sound) elements. The first cluster has been described for you. Fill in the information for the remaining three clusters.

馬　情　嗎　袁　瑪　爸　遠　請
巴　轅　園　遠　把　清　青　媽

CLUSTER 1　　Phonetic: _____袁_____　_____yuán_____
　　　　　　　　　　　　　character　　　　*pinyin*

character	radical	*pinyin*	meaning
轅	車	yuán	cart shaft
遠	辶	yuǎn	far
園	囗	yuán	garden

CLUSTER 2　　Phonetic: _____　_____
　　　　　　　　　　　　　character　　　　*pinyin*

character	radical	*pinyin*	meaning
瑪		mǎ	agate

CLUSTER 3　　Phonetic: _____巴_____　_____bā_____
　　　　　　　　　　　　　character　　　　*pinyin*

character	radical	*pinyin*	meaning
把		bǎ	grasp, hold
		ba	(particle marking suggestion)

CLUSTER 4　　Phonetic: _____青_____　_____qīng_____
　　　　　　　　　　　　　character　　　　*pinyin*

character	radical	*pinyin*	meaning
情		qíng	feelings
清		qīng	clear

Note how each of the phonetic components is a fair indication of the pronunciation of the character, while the radical component provides a clue to the meaning of the character. Many (but not all) Chinese characters are made up of such radical and phonetic parts. Not all of these parts, however, are as accurate in representing sound and meaning as the ones presented here.

SEGMENT A: Locations and directions.

1. Write the *pinyin* for each of the characters below.

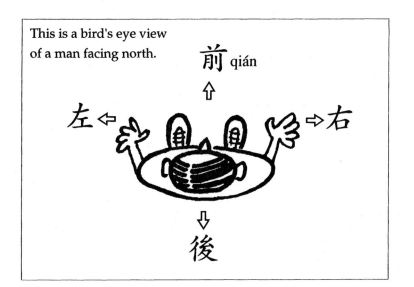

This is a bird's eye view of a man facing north.

前 qián

左 ⇦   ⇨ 右

⇩
後

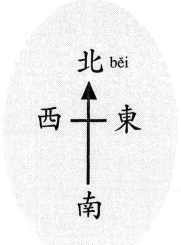

北 běi

西 ⟵┼⟶ 東

南

進來／去 ⟶ 裡頭 lǐtou ⟶ 出來／去
jìnlai

外頭

2. This sign is posted at an underpass at the Great Wall. ➡

Fill in the blanks in the English equivalent.

"Please walk on the _____.
_____ stop _____ the passage."

Fill in the blanks in the *pinyin* version.

_____ kào _____ xíng.
Dòng nèi _____ tíng.

3. This sign is posted at the Imperial Palace in Beijing. ➡

Fill in the blank in the English equivalent.

"Visitors stop (here). (No admittance.)
Please go through the _____ gate."

Fill in the blanks in the *pinyin* version.

Yóu _____ zhǐ bù.

_____ _____ _____ _____

⬅ 4. "Right turn prohibited."
　　　Jìnzhǐ yòu zhuǎn.

Fill in the English below.

jìnzhǐ: to prohibit, forbid
yòu:　_____
zhuǎn: to _____

← 5. Guess which of the following is indicated by this sign.

"Go to the right side ⬜ to buy tickets."

⬜ to line up."

⬜ to enter."

Fill in the blanks in the *pinyin* equivalent.

_____ _____ _____ cè gòu piào.

6. According to the sign below, the _____ is located to the _____ of where you are located.

Fill in the blanks in *pinyin*:

_____ _____ wǎng _____.

a

b

7. Match the English captions with the signs on these two pages by writing the appropriate letter in four of the boxes below.

This way up.	
This way down.	
This way upstairs.	
This way downstairs.	
Entrance.	
Exit.	

c

d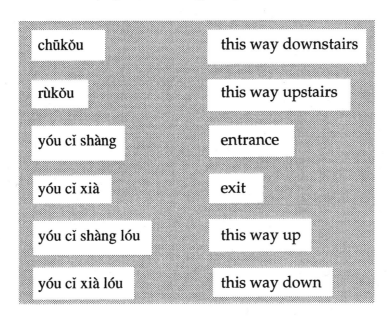

Match the *pinyin* and the English.

chūkǒu	this way downstairs
rùkǒu	this way upstairs
yóu cǐ shàng	entrance
yóu cǐ xià	exit
yóu cǐ shàng lóu	this way up
yóu cǐ xià lóu	this way down

8. Read aloud with a partner.

<u>Situation 1</u>

Two classmates are walking together to the bus-stop.

小紅：你家在哪兒？   Where is your house?

小黃：在北邊兒。   In the north.

小紅：北邊兒甚麼地方？   Where in the north?

小黃：中山路那兒。   Over on Sun Yatsen Avenue.

小紅：房號多少？   What's the house number?

小黃：你為甚麼要問？   Why do you ask?

小紅：沒甚麼，我只是問問。   No reason, I'm just asking.

<u>Situation 2</u>

A mother looks out the window and sees her young son playing outside.

媽媽：阿毛啊，你進來！   Oh Ah-mao, come inside!

阿毛：我來了！   I'm coming!

媽媽：快一點呀！   Hurry up!

阿毛：來了，來了。   Coming, coming.

<u>Situation 3</u>

A teacher looks quizzically at a student who is setting up chairs for a skit.

老師：誰坐在左邊兒，   Who's sitting on the left, and who's
      誰坐在右邊兒？   sitting on the right?

陳覺：我坐在左邊兒，   I'm sitting on the left, Li is
      小李坐在右邊兒。   sitting on the right.

Situation 4

A wife and husband arrive at home together.

太太：你先進去吧，我就　　　　You go in first, I'll be right in.
　　　來了。

先生：沒關係，我等你。　　　　It doesn't matter, I'll wait for you.

太太：你不用等我。進　　　　　You don't need to wait for me. Just go
　　　去就是了。　　　　　　　in.

媽媽：怎麼了？　　　　　　　　What's going on?

太太：你別問我，你先　　　　　Don't ask, go in first.
　　　進去。

9. Summary. For each word in English on the following page, fill in the *pinyin* , the corresponding number for traditional characters and the corresponding letter for simplified characters.

left			
right			
in front			
behind			
north			
south			
east			
west			
to enter (lit.)			
to exit			
an entrance	rùkǒu		
an exit			
No admittance.	Yóurén zhǐbù.		
prohibited	jìnzhǐ		
to buy tickets (lit.)	gòupiào		
This way down.			
Where do you live?			
What's the house #?			
Why are you asking?			
No reason/nothing's happening.			
Come in!			
I'm coming!			
Hurry up!			
I'll wait for you.			
You don't need to wait.			
What's going on?			
Don't ask.			

1. 遊人止步。
2. 後
3. 由此下。
4. 東
5. 出
6. 你爲甚麼問？
7. 進來！
8. 右
9. 我等你。
10. 你家在哪兒？
11. 怎麼了？
12. 南
13. 來了！
14. 房號多少？
15. 你不用等。
16. 左
17. 禁止
18. 入口
19. 前
20. 你別問。
21. 購票
22. 西
23. 入
24. 快一點兒！
25. 出口
26. 沒甚麼。
27. 北

a. 你为什么问？
b. 禁止
c. 我等你。
d. 来了！
e. 怎么了？
f. 购票
g. 你不用等。
h. 入口
i. 游人止步。
j. 左
k. 出
l. 入
m. 你别问。
n. 进来！
o. 出口
p. 西
q. 没什么。
r. 由此下。
s. 快一点儿！
t. 南
u. 北
v. 后
w. 房号多少？
x. 你家在哪儿？
y. 右
z. 前
aa. 东

10. Practice writing.

外	夕 wài outside	

頭	头	頁 / 、 tóu head, top, first

進	进	辶 jìn enter

出	凵 chū go/come out, exit

北	匕 běi north	

邊	边	辶 biān side, edge

等	竹 děng to wait	

鐘	钟	金 / 钅 zhōng bell, clock, o'clock

房	戶 fáng house, room	

左	工 zuǒ left

右	口 yòu right

11. You were to meet a friend at his house. You waited an hour, but he didn't show up. Transcribe the following note (to tape to his door) into characters (some are provided).

Xiǎo Wáng:

Wǒ zài wàitou 等 le nǐ yíge zhōngtóu. Nǐ zěnme méi lái? 今晚 qǐng gěi wǒ dǎ diànhuà.

(Your name)

_____

_____

_____

_____

_____

_____

Now pretend you are 小王. Write an apologetic note to your friend, explaining what happened (make something up, based on what you know how to say). Promise to call tonight.

_____

_____

_____

_____

_____

　　　　　　　　　　　　　　　　　王明 _____

SEGMENT B: Rooms in a house.

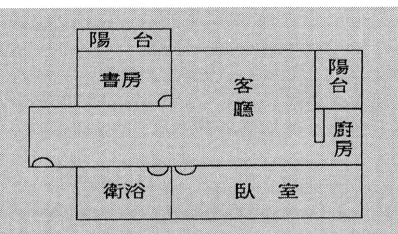

陽台
書房
客廳
陽台
廚房
衛浴
臥室

服務專線：
391-2266
391-1104

ERA 經紀人
黃惠民
執照號碼：R800011

1. The apartment being advertised features two balconies (yángtái), a living room (kètīng), a bedroom (wòshì), a study (shūfáng), a kitchen (chúfáng), and a bathroom (wèiyù). Label each Chinese term in the layout with its English equivalent.

√What is the name of the realtor handling this sale? Answer: _____ Huìmín
√Circle and label the characters zhízhào hàomǎ meaning "license number."
√"Realtor" is jīngjìrén. Circle and label these characters.

2. Read aloud with a partner.

<u>Situation 1</u>

Two brothers are at home.

哥哥：爸爸在哪兒？		Where is Dad?
弟弟：到外頭去了。		He went outside.
哥哥：外頭甚麼地方？		Where outside?
弟弟：可能到花園裡去了。		Maybe he went into the garden.

Situation 2

A teenage girl is in the bathroom washing her hair. Her mother calls to her.

媽媽： 小明，你的朋友來了！   Xiao Ming, your friend is here!

小明： 喔，她在哪兒？   Oh, where is she?

媽媽： 在客廳裡坐着呢！   Sitting in the living room!

小明： 叫她到洗澡間裡來吧！   Tell her to come to the bathroom!

Situation 3

It is naptime, after lunch. A little girl is falling asleep at the table.

爸爸： 阿紅，別在那裡睡着了。   A-Hong, don't fall asleep there. Go with
　　　　跟姐姐到臥室裡去睡。   your sister to the bedroom to sleep.

阿紅： 嗯。   Okay.

Situation 4

Three young people are at home, awaiting the arrival of dinner guests.

二哥： 小弟，到樓上去叫大哥。   Younger brother, go upstairs and call
　　　　　　　　　　　　　　　　　　 Eldest Brother.

弟弟： 叫他做甚麼？   What should I call him for?

二哥： 一起到外頭去。   Let's go outside together.

弟弟： 去哪兒？   Where are we going?

二哥： 到前院去等客人。   To the front yard to wait for the guests.

3. On the following page is a note from Aihui, informing her friend Mary that arrangements for their holiday at the vacation house have all been made. On the plan below, label each of the rooms in English, based on the contents of the letter.

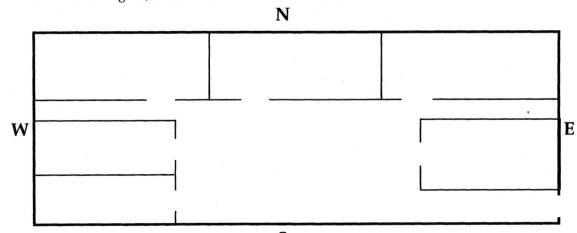

亲爱的 Mary,

你好！今年暑假的房子订好了,向你介绍一下各房间的位置：你跟你妹妹住在东北边的卧房,这间卧房西边还有一间卧房, 给Michiko 住 。这两间卧房的西边有一个洗澡间, 你们两个人合用。洗澡间南边是书房,书房南边是客厅, 也就是房子的西南角。厨房非常大, 一进门就在你的右边。厨房跟书房中间是饭厅。

不多写了, 再见吧！

爱惠

三月三日

4. Summary. For each word in English below, fill in the *pinyin*, the corresponding number for traditional characters and the corresponding letter for simplified characters.

living room			
dining room			
study			
bedroom			
bathroom			
kitchen			
balcony	*yángtái*		
license number	*zhízhào hàomǎ*		
realtor	*jīngjìrén*		
garden			
front yard			
and, with			

1.	廚房	a.	阳台
2.	飯廳	b.	客厅
3.	臥室／房	c.	书房
4.	前院	d.	经纪人
5.	客廳	e.	花园
6.	跟	f.	厨房
7.	經紀人	g.	前院
8.	陽台	h.	洗澡间
9.	洗澡間	i.	饭厅
10.	書房	j.	执照号码
11.	執照號碼	k.	卧室／房
12.	花園	l.	跟

5. Practice writing.

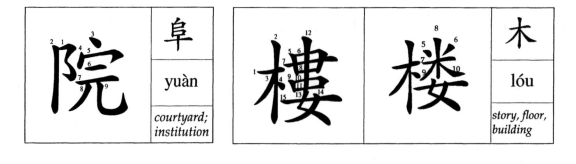

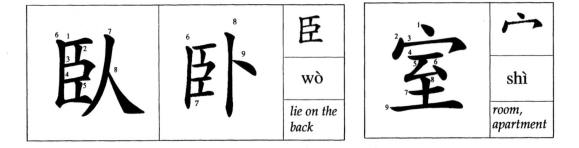

6. You are writing a brief description of your house in a letter to a penfriend. Fill in the blank spaces below by transcribing the *pinyin* into characters.

Wǒ jiāli yǒu wǔ jiān fángjiān. Fàntīng zài qiántou. Fàntīng yòubian shì chúfáng, fàntīng hòubian shì shūfáng. Wòshì zài shūfáng hòutou. Shūfáng zuǒbiān shì xǐzǎojiān. Qiányuàn zài xǐzǎojiān qiántou.

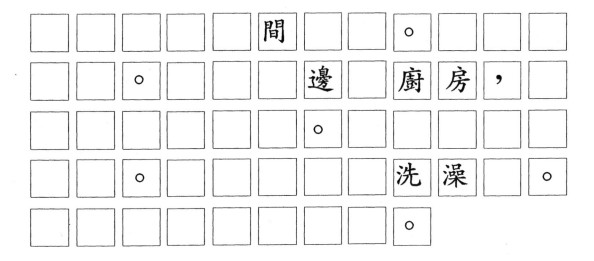

Based on the passage you have written, label in English the rooms in the layout of the house below.

Front

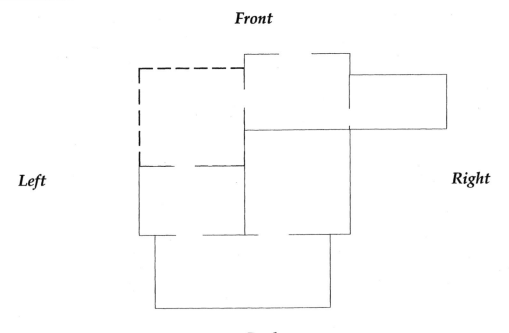

Left

Right

Back

7. Write a prose description (in characters) of the layout of a house, based on the plan below.

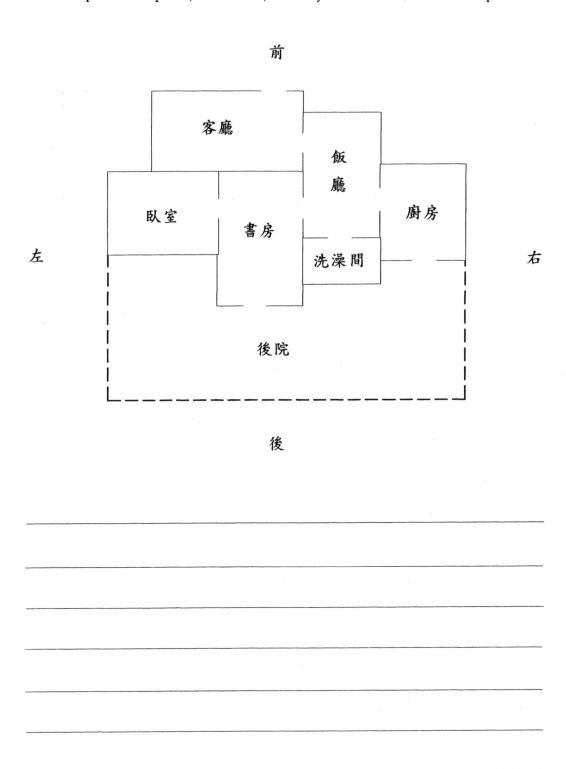

前

客廳

飯廳

臥室　　書房　　　廚房

洗澡間

左　　　　　　　　　　　　　右

後院

後

SEGMENT C: Items in a room.

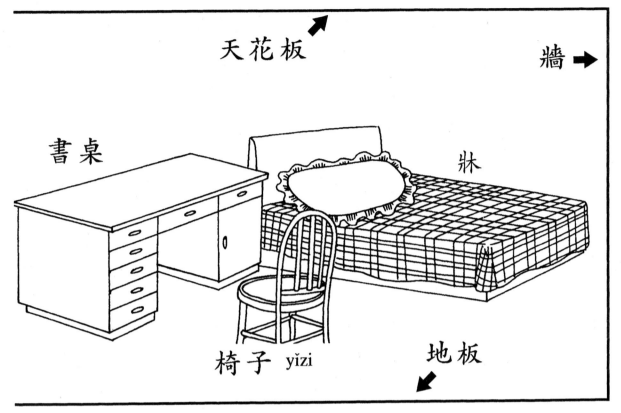

天花板   牆 ➡

書桌   牀

椅子 yǐzi   地板

1. Label the character terms provided above with their pīnyīn equivalents.

2. Read aloud with a partner.

Situation 1

Two sisters are in their room in the afternoon, after a heavy lunch. One has fallen asleep on the other's bed.

陳姐：過去一點兒，我也要睡。 Move over, I want to sleep too.

陳妹：嗯。 Mmm.

陳姐：快過去呀！這是我 Hurry up and move! This is my
　　　的床啊！ bed!

Situation 2

A couple is at an evening reception at a school.

陳中方：書桌旁邊的那個人 Who's the person next to the desk?
　　　　是誰？

李冰心：是王老師的男朋友。 It's Teacher Wang's boyfriend.

Situation 3

Zhang Ying visits her friend Wang Three at his home.

張英：哎，你的牀到哪兒
　　　去了？

Hey, where did your bed go?

王三：我們把它賣了。

We sold it!

張英：爲甚麽賣了？

Why did you sell it?

王三：一個人睡太大了。

It was too big for one person.

Situation 4

Two roommates are in their room late one afternoon.

甲：一天看着四面牆，
　　多沒意思。

How boring it is to stare at four walls all day.

乙：你累了，去休息吧。

You're tired. Go rest.

甲：睡下來看天花板
　　也不怎麽好。

Lying down and staring at the ceiling isn't much better.

3. Below are the layouts of three dormitory rooms, each furnished with a bed and a desk. Match the descriptions provided with the layout of each room by writing the room number in the space marked with a dotted line.

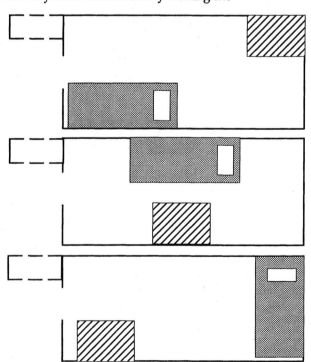

101. 從門口進去，牀在左邊，
　　　書桌在右邊，在牀的
　　　正對面。

102. 牀對着門口，書桌在
　　　門的右邊。

103. 一進去，牀就在右邊兒。
　　　書桌在左邊，在斜對着牀
　　　的角落裡。

4. Summary. For each word in English on the following page, fill in the *pinyin*, the corresponding number for traditional characters and the corresponding letter for simplified characters.

ceiling			
floor			
four walls			
desk			
bed			
uninteresting, boring			
side, next to	*pángbiān*		
doorway			
as soon as you enter			
across (from)			
directly across	*zhèng duìmiàn*		
diagonally across	*xié duìmiàn*		
corner			

1. 沒意思   a. 你一进去
2. 斜對面   b. 天花板
3. 地板   c. 斜对面
4. 你一進去   d. 旁边
5. 牀   e. 角落
6. 角落   f. 四面墙
7. 天花板   g. 地板
8. 對面   h. 书桌
9. 旁邊   i. 对面
10. 四面牆   j. 床
11. 正對面   k. 正对面
12. 門口   l. 没意思
13. 書桌   m. 门口

5. Practice writing.

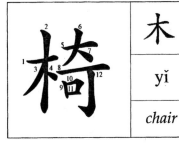

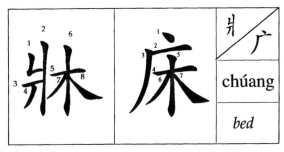

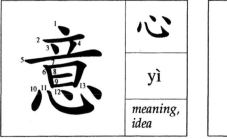

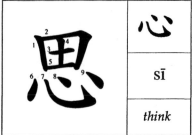

6. Pretend you are living in the dorm room featured below. Write a Chinese character description of its layout.

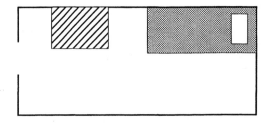

_____

_____

_____

SEGMENT D: Routine activities.

1. Match the health-related slogans below with their English equivalents by filling in the blanks, as in the example.

早起 睡前 飯後 都要刷牙   *c*   *g*   *h*   *e*

飯前 便後 要洗手   ___ ___ ___

好孩子 天天要洗澡   ___ ___

a. you must wash your hands

b. good children

c. upon rising

d. before eating

e. you must brush your teeth

f. after relieving yourself

g. before sleeping

h. after eating

i. must bathe every day

2. Read aloud with a partner.

Situation 1

Two children are waiting for their father to come out of the bathroom.

老三 ： 爸爸怎麼還沒出來呢？

Why hasn't Dad come out yet?

老四 ： 他還在洗臉刷牙。

He's still washing his face and brushing his teeth.

Situation 2

Two teachers are chatting after class.

白 ： 你們家誰做飯？

Who cooks in your house?

馬 ： 平常我做，有的時候

我弟弟做。

Normally I do. Sometimes my little brother does.

Situation 3

Two roommates talk one evening.

甲：你跟我們一塊兒去看
　　電影嗎？

Are you going to the movies with us?

乙：不，我有功課要做。

No, I have homework to do.

甲：你眞是個好學生。

You really are a good student.

Situation 4

A child is on the telephone to her mother.

小美：媽，您幾點回家？

Mom, when will you come home?

媽媽：六點左右。

Around six o'clock.

小美：媽早點回來吧。
　　　我等着您。

Come home sooner, Mom. I'm waiting for you.

媽媽：我六點就回來了。
　　　有好東西給你吃啊！

I'll be home at six (and that's soon). I have something good for you to eat!

3. Write the order in which the daily activities listed in English below are carried out by the woman and man, based on their statements.

a. wash face
b. eat breakfast
c. go to sleep
d. leave the house
e. brush teeth
f. eat dinner
g. change clothes
h. read
i. do homework
j. take a bath
k. get up

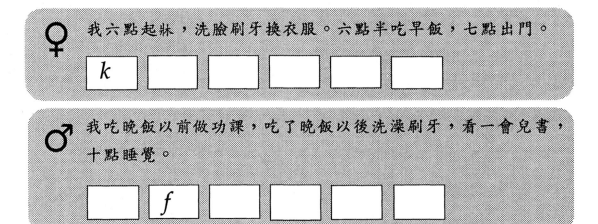

♀ 我六點起牀，洗臉刷牙換衣服。六點半吃早飯，七點出門。

k					

♂ 我吃晚飯以前做功課，吃了晚飯以後洗澡刷牙，看一會兒書，十點睡覺。

	f				

4. Summary. For each word in English on the following page, fill in the *pinyin*, the corresponding number for traditional characters and the corresponding letter for simplified characters.

English	pinyin		
get up, rise			
wash face			
brush teeth			
change clothes	*huàn yīfu*		
defecate	*dàbiàn*		
urinate			
bathe			
cook			
do homework			
leave home			
return home			
normally, usually	*píngcháng*		

1. 洗澡   a. 刷牙
2. 出門   b. 做饭
3. 刷牙   c. 做功课
4. 平常   d. 洗脸
5. 起牀   e. 大便
6. 做功課   f. 平常
7. 大便   g. 出门
8. 回家   h. 小便
9. 做飯   i. 回家
10. 小便   j. 洗澡
11. 洗臉   k. 换衣服
12. 換衣服   l. 起床

5. Practice writing.

功 力
gōng
merit, skill, achievement

課 课 言/讠
kè
subject, class

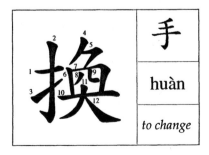

換 手
huàn
to change

門 门 門/门
mén
door, gate

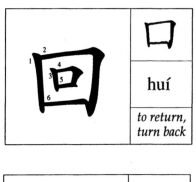

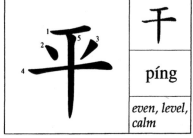

6. Use as many of the terms below as you can to describe your daily schedule of activities.

起牀　　做功課　　看電視　　看書　　出門

睡覺　　吃中飯　　吃晚飯　　吃早飯　回家

_____

_____

_____

SEGMENT A: Items in a classroom.

1. Draw lines to match the Chinese titles on the left with their English equivalents on the right.

XĪNHUÁ ZÌDIĂN

新华字典

世界地图册

筆記本

普通話課本

World Atlas

Pǔtōnghuà Textbook

New China Dictionary

Notebook

Circle and label the Chinese characters for the following.

zìdiǎn   dìtú   kèběn   bǐjìběn

2. Read aloud with a partner.

<u>Situation 1</u>

Chinese class has just begun.

教師：請把課本和字典拿出來。

Please take out your textbooks and dictionaries.

同學：老師，我忘了帶字典。

Teacher, I forgot to bring my dictionary.

教師：怎麼又忘了帶呀？

How come you forgot it again!

同學：老師，我前天沒忘啊！

Teacher, I didn't forget it day before yesterday!

<u>Situation 2</u>

Two classmates are talking in a corridor at school.

甲：我的筆記本不見了。

My notebook is missing.

乙：沒在你的書包裡嗎？

Isn't it in your bookbag?

甲：沒有，不知道放哪兒了。

No, I don't know where I put it.

乙：你今天用過嗎？

Did you use it today?

甲：用過。上中文課的時候
　　用過。

I did. I used it in Chinese class.

乙：啊？今天沒上中文課呀！

Huh? We didn't have Chinese class today!

甲：哦，對了。那還在家裡。

Oh, that's right. Then it's still at home.

<u>Situation 3</u>

Wang and Li are working together in a classroom after school.

王：北海在哪兒？

Where is the North Sea?

李：你到地圖上去找吧。

Why don't you go look for it on the map.

王：地圖在哪兒？

Where's the map?

乙：那兒不就是嗎？

Isn't it right over there?

王：哪兒？

Where?

乙：你這個人，甚麼也
　　看不見。在那兒！

You, you can't see anything. Over there!

王：哪兒？

Where?

乙：那兒！那兒！
　　（過去）這兒！

There! There! (going over) Here!

王：哦。多謝。

Oh. Thanks a lot.

Situation 4

A parent and child are looking at a poster.

小黃：我喜歡那張海報。
　　　畫得真好。

I like that poster. I think it's really well drawn.

老黃：好甚麼。我覺得一
　　　點也不好。

What's so good about it. I don't think it's good at all.

3. Match the request on the left with the object requested on the right.

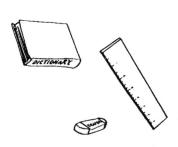

a. 請借我你的筆用一下。

b. 請把你的字典借給我用一下。

c. 我可以借一下你的書嗎？

d. 你可以借我幾張紙嗎？

e. 你能把筆記本借給我看看嗎？

f. 請把你的地圖冊借我一下。

g. 我可以借一下你的課本嗎？

4. Summary. For each word in English below, fill in the *pinyin* , the corresponding number for traditional characters and the corresponding letter for simplified characters.

New China			
dictionary			
world	*shìjiè*		
map			
atlas	*dìtú cè*		
textbook			
Common Speech (Mandarin Chinese)	*Pǔtōnghuà*		
notebook			
take out			
forget to bring			
again (of past action)	*yòu*		
be missing			
bookbag			
poster			
lend, borrow	*jiè*		
(prep. marking the direct object of a verb)	*bǎ*		
put, place			
to use			

1. 地圖册   a. 新华
2. 借   b. 课本
3. 又   c. 世界
4. 世界   d. 不见了
5. 字典   e. 书包
6. 普通話   f. 海报
7. 拿出來   g. 借
8. 書包   h. 笔记本
9. 用   i. 把
10. 把   j. 普通话
11. 忘了帶   k. 地图
12. 筆記本   l. 用
13. 課本   m. 放
14. 放   n. 忘了带
15. 海報   o. 字典
16. 地圖   p. 又
17. 不見了   q. 拿出来
18. 新華   r. 地图册

5. Practice writing.

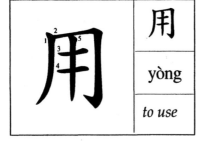

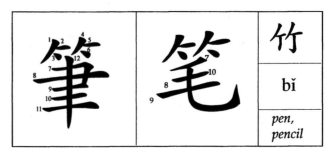

借	人 jiè lend, borrow	圖 图	口 tú map, picture
忘	心 wàng forget	帶 带	巾 dài take, bring
包	勹 bāo bag, package	記 记	言 / 讠 jì remember, write down
把	手 bǎ hold, grasp; (marker of direct object)	海	水 hǎi sea; extra large
放	攵 fàng put, place	典	八 diǎn standard work

我今天忘了帶字典和課本。我能借用一下你的嗎？

6. A classmate passes you this note. ➡

You, however, have also forgotten yours. Write a note back, explaining the situation and apologizing.

_____

_____

_____

_____

Write a note to another classmate, asking to borrow one or more of the following.
√ an atlas
√ his/her notebook
√ a red pen

_____

_____

_____

_____

SEGMENT B: School routine.

1. The following is a representation of one portion of a Chinese bookstore, where books are displayed in sections devoted to different topic areas. Match the English equivalents of the topic areas (in the rectangles) with the Chinese by writing the appropriate numbers in the circles.

1. math   2. science   3. history   4. foreign languages
5. geography   6. physical education

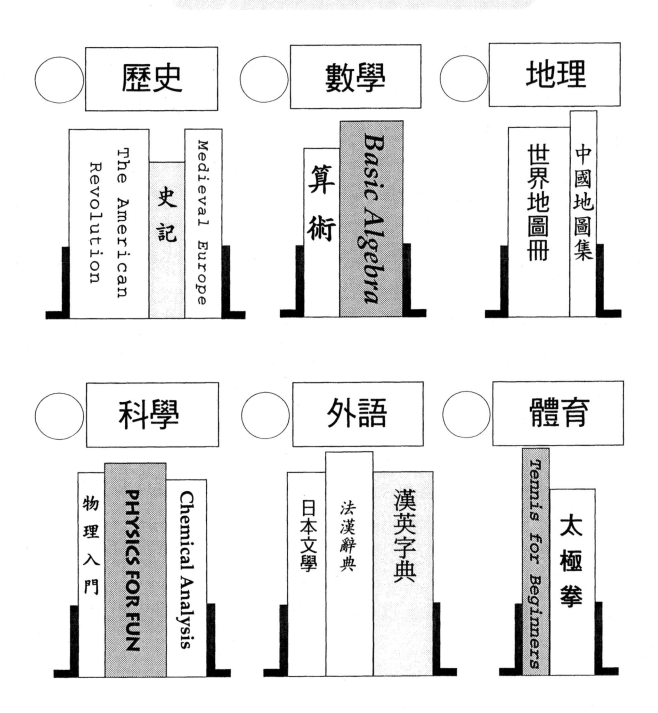

2. Below is the graduation certificate of a young scholar from the People's Republic of China. Scan through the translation of it that follows, and fill in the blanks with information drawn from the Chinese text.

毕 业 证 书

学生 **郝平** 系 **山东省烟台市** 人，性别 **男**

于 **一九五九** 年 **九** 月 **十五** 日生，一九七八 年 十 月至一九八二 年 七 月

在本校 **历史学** 系 **世界史** 专业学习，完成 四 年制

本科教学计划规定的学习任务，成绩合格，准予毕业。

北京大学校长 **张龙翔**

一九八二年七月　　日

毕证字第 **821323** 号

Graduation Certificate

The student HAO PING, a native of SHANDONG PROVINCE, YANTAI CITY, a male, born on
_____ , who from October, 1978, until July, 1982, attended the
_____ department of this university, specializing in _____ ,
has completed a FOUR-year curriculum of required courses of learning with satisfactory scores,
and is permitted to graduate.

President, Peking University
ZHANG LONGXIANG

July, 1982

Certificate # 821323

3. Read the information below and write in Arabic numerals how much each course indicated by the pictures on the right is worth in each semester.

學分 = credit hour

1. 第一個學期數學是五個學分。

2. 第二個學期中文是四個學分。

3. 第一個學期歷史是三個學分。

4. 第二個學期地理是三個學分。

5. 第一個學期體育是三個學分。

6. 第一個學期中文是三個學分。

7. 第二個學期社會學是六個學分。

8. 第一個學期科學是五個學分。

9. 第二個學期數學是兩個學分。

10. 第一個學期地理是兩個學分。

11. 第二個學期科學是三個學分。

12. 第二個學期歷史是三個學分。

13. 第二個學期體育是兩個學分。

14. 第一個學期社會學是一個學分。

Sem. 1	Course	Sem. 2

4. Following are two excerpts from the 1991 (remember, by the R.O.C. calendar 1991 = 1911 + 80) National Taiwan University academic calendar, as well as a portion of an American student's letter home. Fill in the blanks in the letter based on information you find in the calendar.

Wow is it hot here! I've been going down to the campus and looking up professors I hope to work with. Many are back now, since the semester has officially begun, although technically summer vacation isn't over yet. Course selection begins on _____, and classes start on _____, a Saturday! Then we'll be in session until January _____. Exams follow and last until _____. I've been thinking of going to Hong Kong over the winter break, since we'll be off for nearly a month, from _____ until _____. I hear it'll be really cold. Will Hao Ping will be there then, do you know?

• •

Wouldn't you know they cancelled my flight back to Taipei and I missed the first day of class, on February _____. Good thing there's another holiday this term, from _____ until _____. I think I'll just stay here and catch up on my studying. Will you come out when the semester's over? The last day of class is _____. Exams go until _____, but I only have two, and chances are they'll be early. Come by June 20, okay?

國立台灣大學八十學年度第一學期行事曆

民國八十年

月	日	星期	事項
8	1	四	本學期開始
9	14	六	暑假結束
9	16	一	選課開始
9	21	六	上課開始
1	14	二	本學期上課最後一天
1	16	四	學期考試開始
1	22	三	學期考試完畢 學期結束
1	23	四	寒假開始
2	22	六	寒假結束

國立台灣大學八十學年度第二學期行事曆

民國八十一年

月	日	星期	事項
2	24	一	本學期開始 選課開始
2	29	六	上課開始
4	1	三	春假（放假三天）
	2	四	
	3	五	
6	15	一	本學期上課最後一天
6	17	三	學期考試開始
6	23	二	學期考試完畢
6	27	六	學期結束 暑假開始

5. The following is a participant's namebadge for a teachers' workshop on student advising. Circle the characters corresponding to the items below, and draw lines to match them.

七十九學年度
『導師輔導工作研討會』
★ ★ ★ ★ ★ ★ ★ ★ ★ ★ ★ ★ ★ ★ ★ ★
台灣大學外文系
史嘉琳

• 1990 academic year

• Taiwan University

• Foreign Languages Department

• Shǐ Jiālín (name of participant)

6. Read aloud with a partner.
Situation 1

Two classmates are working on a math problem together.

男生：你眞行。 You are really something.

女生：你這是甚麼意思？ What do you mean by that?

男生：沒甚麼意思…我説 Nothing much...I just mean you are good in
你數學好。 math.

Situation 2

Wang and Li are chatting at the beginning of a new semester.

小王：你這個學期選了 What courses are you taking this semester?
甚麼課？

老李：中文、英文、社會 Chinese, English, sociology, and history.
學、還有歷史。

小王：你只選了四門課嗎？ Are you only taking four courses?

老李：還不夠嗎？你選了 Isn't that enough? How many are you taking?
幾門？

小王：六門。 Six.

Situation 3

Class is just over; the teacher walks out with two students.

教師：　你們暑假去玩嗎？　　Are you going anywhere for summer vacation?

學生一：我回家去。　　I'm going home.

學生二：我哪兒也不去。　　I'm not going anywhere. I'm working at
　　　　我在學校工作。　　school.

Situation 4

Dazhong shows Meiying a photograph of his family.

美英：你母親是做甚麼的？　　What does your mother do?

大中：她是科學家，她做　　She's a scientist; she's doing research.
　　　研究工作。

Situation 5

Two students are getting ready for a soccer game.

張：體育課幾點上課幾　　What time does the physical education class
　　點下課？　　begin and what time does it end?

陳：七點上課九點下課。　　It starts at seven and ends at nine.

Situation 6

Student A attends school X, and meets students B and C, who attend school Y, at a party.

甲：你們學校念書難　　Is it hard studying at your school?
　　不難？

乙：不難，很容易。　　It's not hard, it's very easy.

丙：那麼你為甚麼學　　Then why are you doing badly in your
　　得不好？　　studies?

乙：誰說我學得不好？　　Who says I'm doing badly? I'm doing
　　我學得還可以。　　alright.

7. Below are two copies of a letter written by an American high-school student named Wēiwei, the first addressed to a friend in Taiwan, the second modified for a friend in the PRC. Except for the difference in the addressee and traditional vs. simplified characters, the content of the letters are the same. Read both and highlight all portions you can understand. Note in English as many pieces of information as you can decipher—what classes Wēiwei takes, number of classes a day, etc.

海燕：

　　妳好！時間過得眞快，寒假早已經過去了，一月十九日第二個學期開學了。這個學期我上六門課：英文、數學、科學、外國文學、歷史和地理。我很忙，每天至少有四節課，功課也非常多。我就等着放暑假，咱們兩個又可以見面了。請你來信告訴我你的學習情況。因爲時間關係，不多寫了，就此止筆。

　　　　祝

　　　　　學業進步！

　　　　　　　　　　　　　　葦葦
　　　　　　　　　　　　　　　　三月四日

小白：

　　你好！时间过得真快，寒假早已经过去了，一月十九日第二个学期开学了。这个学期我上六门课：英文、数学、科学、外国文学、历史和地理。我很忙，每天至少有四节课，功课也非常多。我就等着放暑假，咱们两个又可以见面了。请你来信告诉我你的学习情况。因为时间关系，不多写了，就此止笔。

　　　　祝

　　　　　学业进步！

　　　　　　　　　　　　　　苇苇
　　　　　　　　　　　　　　　　三月四日

_____ √ winter break is long past; the 2nd semester began on Jan. 19.

_____

_____

_____

_____

_____

8. Summary. For each word in English below, fill in the *pinyin*, the corresponding number for traditional characters and the corresponding letter for simplified characters.

English	pinyin		
to graduate	bìyè		
school			
department			
literature	wénxué		
history			
mathematics			
geography			
science			
foreign language	wàiyǔ		
physical education			
sign up for a class			
semester			
credit hour			
to begin, start	kāishǐ		
to end, finish	wán		
to end, conclude	jiéshù		
exam, take an exam	kǎoshì		
to be easy			
have a holiday, be on vacation			
winter break			
spring break			
summer vacation			

1. 數學	a. 结束
2. 系	b. 文学
3. 寒假	c. 考试
4. 開始	d. 毕业
5. 選課	e. 暑假
6. 畢業	f. 放假
7. 結束	g. 历史
8. 春假	h. 寒假
9. 考試	i. 完
10. 暑假	j. 学校
11. 地理	k. 体育
12. 外語	l. 数学
13. 放假	m. 学分
14. 容易	n. 选课
15. 學校	o. 学期
16. 學期	p. 科学
17. 完	q. 系
18. 科學	r. 外语
19. 體育	s. 春假
20. 文學	t. 容易
21. 學分	u. 地理
22. 歷史	v. 开始

9. Practice writing.

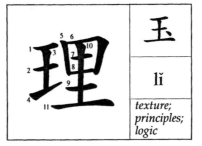

10. Pretend you are the recipient of Wēiwei's note (item 7 above). Write a response, making some brief statements about your own semester.

SEGMENT C: Moving around school.

女生宿舍

辦公室

教室

教室

教室

教室

教室

圖書館

教室

大禮堂

教室

男廁

女廁

教室

1. This is the layout of a hypothetical Chinese school. Label each of the location names in English.

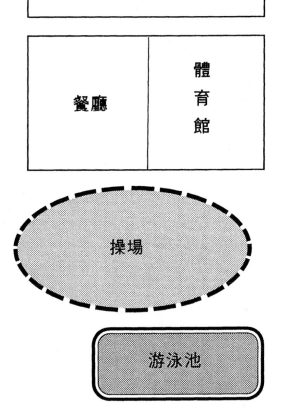

男生宿舍

餐廳

體育館

操場

游泳池

2. This sign is posted just inside the front door of a building on a university campus. What is this building?
Answer:

_____

遊客 yóukè = visitors

止 zhǐ = stop

步 bù = footsteps

Guess what line 2 says.

☐ Please wait here.

☐ No trespassing.

☐ Pick up point.

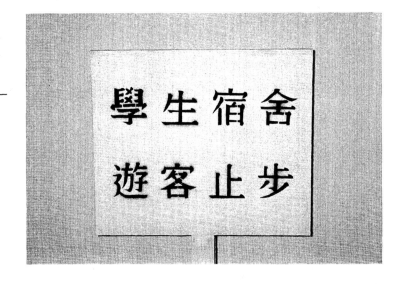

學生宿舍
遊客止步

2. The following are statements made by a student named Yu Xiuming in the course of a school week, about **where** she will be meeting various people. Next to each location indicated, write in *pinyin* the last name of the person she will be meeting.

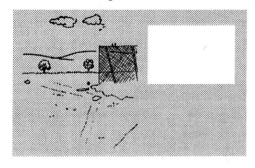

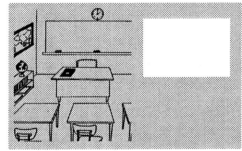

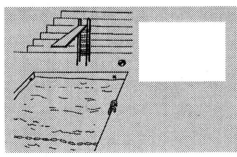

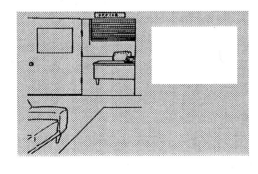

我到體育館去找小李。

我到游泳池去找王大同。

我到女生宿舍去找陳平。

我到男生宿舍去找小白。

我到教室裡去見黃老師。

我到餐廳去等老高。

我到操場去等我爸爸。

我到辦公室去見張校長。

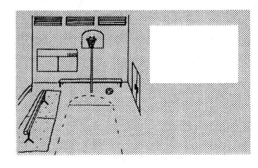

3. Below is a note left on the desk of a student whose first name is Mary, by her friend Méi Fāng. What information does Méi want? What would he like Mary to do, if she can?

玛丽：
　你知道小明在哪个办公室？
知道的话，请给我打个电话。多谢了！

小梅

Mălì:

Transcribe Méi's note into *pinyin*. ➡

_____

_____

_____

Xiǎo Méi

友梅
我在教室裏，若有事請到
那兒去找我．

S

4. This is a note posted by one teacher on another teacher's ⬅ door.

What information does S(tephen) provide? What suggestion does he make?

5. 若 X (ruò X) is the literary way of saying X 的 話 ("if X"). Complete the chart based on the terms used in the two notes on this page.

Literary	Colloquial	English
若有事		*If there is something (you need me for)*
若知道		

6. Read aloud with a partner.

Situation 1

One student finds another waiting outside the school office early in the morning.

甲：你一個人坐在這兒做甚麼？　　　What are you doing, sitting here by yourself?

乙：辦公室還沒開門，我在等人來。　The office hasn't opened yet. I'm waiting for someone to come.

Situation 2

A student walks into a departmental office.

秘書：你找哪一位？　　　Who are you looking for?

學生：馬老師在嗎？　　　Is Teacher Ma here?

秘書：不，教課去了。　　No, she's gone to teach a class.

學生：在哪兒教課？　　　Where is she teaching?

秘書：502號教室。　　　　Classroom 502.

Situation 3

Two students leave class at lunchtime.

張同學：你帶午飯了嗎？　　　Did you bring a lunch?

李同學：沒有。我到餐廳去買。　No. I'll go buy one at the cafeteria.

Situation 4

Three students are through with classes for the day.

甲：咱們回宿舍去吧。　　　Let's go back to the dorm.

乙：等我一會兒，我去一下圖書館。　Wait for me a while, I'm going to stop over at the library.

丙：我跟你一塊兒去。　　　I'll go with you.

甲：你們去圖書館吧。我
　　　一個人先回宿舍去了。　You guys go to the library. I'll go back first to the dorm by myself.

Situation 5

Two male students are chatting.

甲：你今年參加了甚麼球隊？　　What teams did you join this year?

乙：美式足球隊，你呢？　　　The American football team. And you?

甲：我想參加啦啦隊 (lālāduì)。　I'm thinking of joining the cheering squad.

乙：那不是女生的事嗎？　　　Isn't that only for female students?

甲：也有男生參加啊。　　　Male students participate too.

7. Summary. For each word in English below, fill in the *pinyin*, the corresponding number for traditional characters and the corresponding letter for simplified characters.

girls' dormitory			
boys' dormitory			
office			
library			
classroom			
gymnasium			
cafeteria			
sports field			
swimming pool			
look for			
if X	X de huà		
participate			

1. 辦公室　　a. 游泳池
2. 餐廳　　　b. 操場
3. 教室　　　c. 參加
4. 游泳池　　d. 女生宿舍
5. 女生宿舍　e. 图书馆
6. X 的話　　f. 找
7. 圖書館　　g. 体育馆
8. 參加　　　h. 教室
9. 找　　　　i. 男生宿舍
10. 男生宿舍　j. 办公室
11. 體育館　　k. X 的话
12. 操場　　　l. 餐厅

8. Practice writing.

找	手 zhǎo seek, look for
到	刀 dào arrive, reach
宿	宀 sù stay overnight

9. Check off the facilities available at your school.

☐ 宿舍　　☐ 圖書館　　☐ 教室

☐ 餐廳　　☐ 游泳池

| 舍 | 舌 shè a shed, house |

Now write a brief prose description of your school, based on your list and the model provided.

我們學校有一個小小的圖書館，很多間教室，還有一個很大的餐廳。我們只有男生宿舍，沒有女生宿舍，也沒有游泳池。

_____

_____

_____

10. Write a note to a friend, asking her/him to meet you tomorrow at 6 p.m. at the cafeteria.

_____
_____
_____
_____
_____

SEGMENT D: Identifying people at school.

1. This is an excerpt from a directory of personnel at a make-believe school, beginning with the president/principal. Label in *pinyin* all the titles listed.

_____	校長：	孫明夫	電話：5217814
jiàowù zhǔrèn	教務主任：	朱君健	電話：5214508

中文系

_____	主任：	杜學良	電話：5219800
_____	教員：	周江寧	電話：5219802
		楊秀山	電話：5219802
		李秋紅	電話：5213477
		劉仁宗	電話：5213528

英文系

_____	主任：	吳守文	電話：5218864
_____	教員：	羅家福	電話：5216537
		陳大年	電話：5216536
		安峰	電話：5215329
		蘇長壽	電話：5215328

2. To whom is the cautionary sign below addressed? Answer:_____

"You absolutely must take care to guard against traffic accidents!"

3. This note is posted on a teacher's desk. Who was looking for him? Check one.

☐ school president   ☐ dean   ☐ department chair

☐ fellow teacher   ☐ student

系主任找你有事.

4. Read aloud with a partner.

Situation 1

A student seeks advice from a teacher.

學生：老師，我明年開始不再上數
　　　學課行嗎？

Teacher, is it alright for me to not take math anymore, beginning next year?

老師：不知道。你去問系主任吧。

I don't know. Why don't you go ask the department chair.

學生：我問過了，她也說不知道。

I've asked; she says she doesn't know either.

老師：那你去找教務主任吧。

Then go call on the dean.

Situation 2

Two male students are chatting.

張：李美英和你是親戚嗎？

Is Li Meiying a relative of yours?

李：不是親戚。她和我妹妹
　　是好朋友。

She's not a relative. She's my sister's good friend.

張：你妹妹叫甚麼名字？

What's your sister's name?

李：李真。

Li Zhen.

張：李真不是李校長的女兒嗎？

Isn't Li Zhen Headmaster Li's daughter?

李：對呀！李校長就是我爸爸。

That's right. Headmaster Li is my father.

張：嘿！說了半天你就是校長的
　　兒子。

Ha! After all this time, (it turns out) you're the headmaster's son.

<u>Situation 3</u>

Two students are trying to check some books out of the library.

甲： 前面那個人大概就是
　　 圖書館員。

That person up ahead is probably the librarian.

乙： 不，他是個學生。

No, he's a student.

甲： 這兒有圖書館員嗎？

<u>Is</u> there a librarian here?

乙： 當然有，只是不知道
　　 是哪位。

Of course there is...I just don't know who it is.

5. Summary. For each word in English below, fill in the *pinyin*, the corresponding number for traditional characters and the corresponding letter for simplified characters.

friend			
department chair			
president/principal			
dean			
Chinese department			
instructor			
probably, most likely	*dàgài*		
librarian			
of course			

1. 中文系　　a. 图书馆员

2. 大概　　　b. 当然

3. 系主任　　c. 教员

4. 當然　　　d. 校长

5. 圖書館員　e. 系主任

6. 校長　　　f. 朋友

7. 教員　　　g. 中文系

8. 朋友　　　h. 教务主任

9. 教務主任　i. 大概

6. Practice writing.

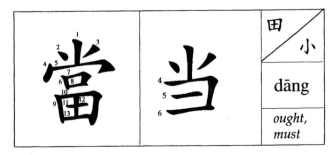

| 朋 | 月
péng
friend | 友 | 又
yǒu
friend | 概 | 木
gài
all, general |

7. Pretend you have a friend named Wú Jūn who needs some information about the people at your school for a project he is doing, and asks you the following questions in a note.

你們學校校長姓甚麼？是男的還是女的？多大歲數了？是哪兒的人？

你們學校有中文系嗎？系主任是誰？有幾位教中文的老師？請你告訴我他們的姓名。

多謝。

吳君

94.12.24

Write a note responding to Wú Jūn 's questions, based on your own school.

_____

_____

_____

_____

_____

_____

SEGMENT A: Food groups and specific foods.

1. On this and the following page are two sides of a menu from a PRC hotel for foreigners. Circle the Chinese characters for the English terms listed on the right, then fill in their *pinyin* equivalents in the spaces on the left.

Note the following key errors in English:
neiu (menu)
culambor (cucumber)
fried rice with assorted (fried rice with assorted ingredients)
fillet (filet)

pinyin (left)	Menu	English (right)
1. *fáng* *jiān*	房 间 服 务 菜 单 ROOM SERVICE NEIU	1. room
2. _____		2. service
3. _____ *dān*		3. menu
4. _____	沙丁鱼 ·············· ¥ 6.00 Sardines	4. fish
5. _____	鸡沙拉 ·············· ¥ 8.00 Chicken Salad	5. chicken
6. *shā* *lā*	柿子黄瓜沙拉 ········· ¥ 3.00 Tomato Culambor Salad	6. salad
	红菜头沙拉 ········· ¥ 3.00 Beetroot Salad	
7. _____	汤 SOUPS	7. soup
8. _____ *shì*	法式洋葱汤 ········· ¥ 5.50 French onion soup	8. French style
9. *yáng* *cōng*		
10. *nǎi* *yóu*	奶油汤 ·············· ¥ 6.00 Cream soup	10. cream
11. *fān* *qié*	蕃茄汤 ·············· ¥ 6.00 Tomato soup	11. tomato
	主 菜 MAIN COURSES	12. main courses
12. *zhǔ* _____	炸大虾 ······· 每份两个 ¥ 45.00 Deep-fried Prawns	13. prawn
13. *dà* _____		

奶汁烤鱼 ••••••••••••••••••••• ￥21.00
Baked Fish with Cream Sauce

清煎牛里几扒 ••••••••••••••••• ￥20.00
Fried fillet Chop

14. ＿＿ ＿＿ 　　煎猪肉洋葱少司 ••••••••••••• ￥10.00 　　14. pork
Fried Pork Chop with Onion Sauce

15. ＿＿ ＿＿ 　　什锦炒饭 ••••••••••••••••••• ￥6.00 　　15. fried rice
Fried Rice with assorted

三 明 治
SANDWICH

16. ＿＿ ＿＿ 　　克拉巴三明治 ••••••••••••••• ￥10.00 　　16. sandwich
　　zhì　　Club Sandwich

17. ＿＿ *tuǐ*　　火腿三明治 ••••••••••••••••• ￥4.40 　　17. ham
Ham Sandwich

18. *rè* *gǒu*　　热　狗 ••••••••••••••••••• ￥6.00 　　18. hot dog
Hot Dog

点 心
DESSERTS

19. *píng guǒ*　　苹果排 ••••••••••••••••••• ￥3.00 　　19. apple
Apple pie

20. *dàn gāo*　　奶油蛋糕 ••••••••••••••••••• ￥4.00 　　20. cake
Cream cake

2. Which will you do to open this door? Take a guess if you don't know for sure.

推　　　push ☐　　pull ☐

How about this one?

拉　　　push ☐　　pull ☐

3. Until the summer of 1993, staple items such as rice, flour and oil were rationed in the P.R.C. Citizens were issued ration coupons, which they could use to obtain supplies. This is a sample of a ration coupon.

What could you buy with it? Circle one of the items listed.

milk

beef

pork

eggs

4. "Seven Delicacies" Self-service Fire Pot

A fire pot is a Chinese style of eating. A pot of boiling flavored broth is set on the table; diners select portions of raw meats and seafoods, place these in the broth, and remove them when they are cooked to taste. One or more sauces are provided for dipping. Near the conclusion of the meal, vegetables and other ingredients are added to the broth, so that the final course is a wonderful soup.

What are three key ingredients available in these fire pots?

1._____

2._____

3.____*lamb/mutton*____

5. Draw arrows by the Xs to indicate the direction in which these three signs are to be read. Then match the captions to the photos by writing the appropriate letter in the space provided.

a

b

c

jiǎozi (dumplings)
beef noodles

boiled jiǎozi (dumplings)
noodles

breakfast

6. Read aloud with a partner.

Situation 1

Two people are trying to leave a bank.

甲： (推門) 怎麼了…這個門開不開啊！

(pushing the door) What's going on... this door won't open!

乙： 門上寫的是『拉』，可你在推，當然開不開！

What's written on the door is "pull," but you are pushing, of course it won't open!

Situation 2

Zhang and Wang sit down in a Chinese restaurant. Wang is newly arrived from overseas.

張： 我來一個湯麵。你叫甚麼？

I'll have a soup noodle. What will you order?

王： 我要一個沙拉…

I'll have a salad...

張： 這兒不賣沙拉呀！

They don't sell salad here!

王： 不賣沙拉？

Don't sell salad?

張： 當然吶！這兒只有中餐，沒有西餐。

Of course not! There's only Chinese food here, no Western food.

王： 哪兒能買到沙拉呢？

Where can I buy salad?

張： 附近 (fùjìn) 有家麥當勞，那兒大概能買到三明治、熱狗、沙拉甚麼的。

There is a McDonald's nearby. There you can probably buy sandwiches, hot dogs, salad, etc.

Situation 3

It is dinnertime in a Chinese restaurant.

甲： 怎麼樣？吃甚麼？

How about it? What shall we have?

乙： 來個雞或鴨吧。

Let's have a chicken or a duck (dish).

甲： 甚麼樣的雞或鴨？

What kind of chicken or duck?

乙： 甚麼樣的都行。然後再叫個魚或蝦。

Anything will do. And then let's order a fish or shrimp.

甲： 甚麼樣的魚或蝦？

What kind of fish or shrimp?

乙： 你說吧。

You decide.

甲： 好吧。那麼…

Okay. In that case...

乙： 別忘了叫青菜。

Don't forget to order a vegetable.

甲： 你慢點兒好不好！

Would you please slow down!

Situation 4

A wife and husband are at the dinner table.

女： 多吃豬肉牛肉對身體不好。

Eating too much pork and beef is not good for your health.

男： 那怎麼辦？牛肉還沒甚麼關係，可是我最愛吃豬肉。

So then what? Beef doesn't matter as much, but I love pork best of all.

女： 吃是可以吃，只是最好少吃一點兒。

You can eat some, but it'd be best to eat less of it.

男： 不吃肉吃甚麼呢？

What shall we eat if we can't eat meat?

女： 吃魚、青菜、水果、還有豆腐。

We can eat fish, vegetables, fruit, and tofu.

7. Summary. For each word in English below, fill in the *pinyin*, the corresponding number for traditional characters and the corresponding letter for simplified characters.

English	pinyin		
menu			
soup			
main course	zhǔ cài		
chicken			
duck			
fish			
shrimp, prawn			
pork			
lamb, mutton	yángròu		
vegetables	qīngcài		
tofu	dòufu		
jiaozi, dumplings			
soup noodles			
fried rice			
sandwich	sānmíngzhì		
hot dog	règǒu		
salad	shālā		
cake	dàngāo		
apple	píngguǒ		
fruit			
Chinese food			
Western food			
breakfast			
push	tuī		
pull	lā		

1. 鴨
2. 三明治
3. 豬肉
4. 中餐
5. 青菜
6. 早點
7. 菜單
8. 蘋果
9. 餃子
10. 西餐
11. 主菜
12. 湯麵
13. 熱狗
14. 拉
15. 魚
16. 蛋糕
17. 推
18. 湯
19. 水果
20. 羊肉
21. 豆腐
22. 沙拉
23. 雞
24. 炒飯
25. 蝦，大蝦

a. 青菜
b. 主菜
c. 推
d. 菜单
e. 饺子
f. 鱼
g. 猪肉
h. 热狗
i. 水果
j. 拉
k. 汤
l. 鸡
m. 鸭
n. 虾，大虾
o. 豆腐
p. 汤面
q. 早点
r. 沙拉
s. 三明治
t. 炒饭
u. 苹果
v. 羊肉
w. 西餐
x. 蛋糕
y. 中餐

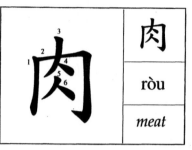

6. Practice writing.

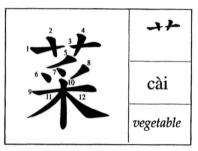

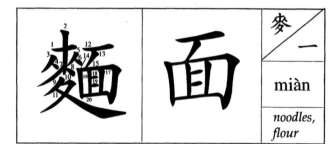

8. A friend will be cooking a meal for you, and has asked about your preferences. Briefly describe what you do and do not like to eat.

SEGMENT B: Style of preparation.

1. Write the *pinyin* for each character accompanying the illustrations below.

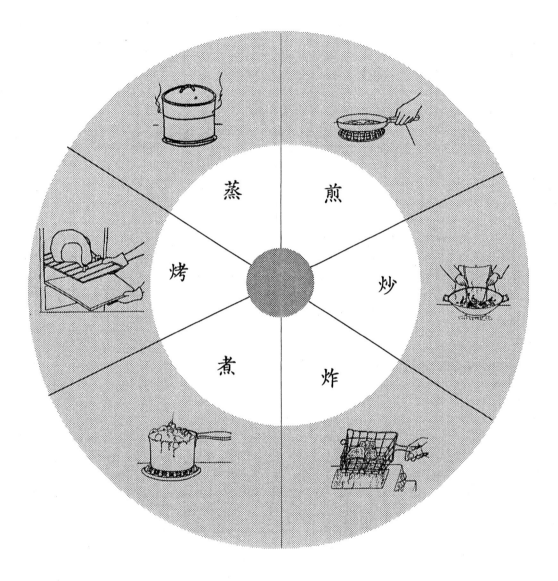

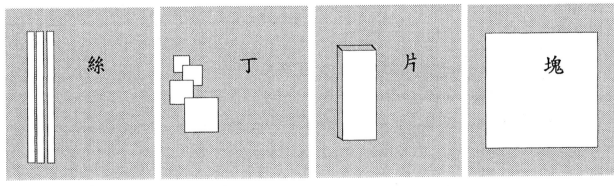

2. This is an October 25 ad for an American fast food franchise in Taiwan.

肯德基............
悅賓特餐
2塊炸雞 • 1份(M)薯條(原價96元)
特價 **80**元

即日起至10月31日止
至肯德基購買悅賓特餐
即可參加15部三陽機車抽獎，另
有8000多個驚喜獎品等您來拿！

Write the name of the franchise: _____

What will 80¥ buy? Answer: _____ & a medium bag of french fries.
Circle and label the characters that tell you this.

Circle and label the terms yuánjià (original price) and tèjià (special price).

Circle and label the terms "special meal."

Circle and label the term Kěndéjī. What do you think it means?

For what period of time is this advertised special available?

3. The following items appear on the menus of a variety of restaurants in Hong Kong. Place each on the most appropriate "table" by writing the letter in the space provided. (The asterisked items are suitable on two tables. Place them on both.)

a. 炸豆腐　　　　　h. 清蒸魚

b. 炒肉絲　　　　　i. 炸大蝦 *

c. 煎雞蛋　　　　　j. 牛肉炒麵

d. 炒雞丁　　　　　k. 烤牛肉

e. 炸雞塊 *

f. 煮雞蛋

g. 青菜炒魚片

Chinese lunch or dinner

American breakfast

American lunch or dinner

4. Read aloud with a partner.

Situation 1

Three friends meet for dinner at a Chinese restaurant.

甲： 我想嘗嘗 chángcháng 這兒的魚。 — I'd like to try the fish here.

乙： 甚麼樣的魚？ — What kind of fish?

丙： 炒魚片，炸魚塊，清蒸全魚⋯ — Stir-fried fish slices, deep fried fish chunks, steamed whole fish...

甲： 你們説呢？ — What do you say (suggest)?

乙： 我喜歡炸的⋯ — I like deep fried food...

丙： 炸的對身體不好。 — Fried food is not good for the health.

甲：那麼就吃蒸的吧。　　　　　Then let's have something steamed.

乙：全魚不很貴嗎？　　　　　　Isn't whole fish very expensive?

丙：是嗎？那麼我們吃魚片吧。　Is it? In that case let's have fish slices.

乙：行。　　　　　　　　　　　Alright.

甲：炒魚片。好吧。　　　　　　Stir-fried fresh fish slices. Okay then.

Situation 2

A Chinese student is introducing a foreign student to his first taste of Chinese food. There are three dishes on the table.

甲：這是甚麼？　　　　　　　　What is this?

乙：肉絲。　　　　　　　　　　Meat slivers.

甲：甚麼肉？　　　　　　　　　What kind of meat?

乙：肉就是豬肉。　　　　　　　Meat means pork.

甲：這也是豬肉嗎？　　　　　　Is this pork too?

乙：不，那是雞丁。　　　　　　No, that's diced chicken.

甲：中國人不吃牛肉嗎？　　　　Don't Chinese people eat beef?

乙：吃啊。你看，這就是　　　　We do! Look, this is sliced beef
　　牛肉片。可以嗎？　　　　　(right here). Is it (all this) okay?
　　　　　　　　　　　　　　　(Will it do?)

甲：可以，可以，很好。我　　　It's fine, fine. It's great. I like
　　甚麼都愛吃，你呢？　　　　everything (I like all kinds of food).
　　　　　　　　　　　　　　　How about you?

乙：我也甚麼都能吃，可是　　　I can eat anything too, but I like
　　我最喜歡吃青菜。　　　　　vegetables best.

5. Summary. For each word in English below, fill in the *pinyin*, the corresponding number for traditional characters, and the corresponding letter for simplified characters.

fried chicken			
original price			
special price	*tèjià*		
to, until	*zhǐ*		
to stop, end			
deep fry			
stir fry			
pan fry			
boil, stew			
steam			
whole fish			
be good for the health			
meat slivers			
diced chicken			
sliced meat			
fish slices			
can, may, to be acceptable	*kěyǐ*		

1. 炒
2. 至
3. 肉絲
4. 炸雞
5. 蒸
6. 肉片
7. 止
8. 雞丁
9. 可以
10. 全魚
11. 煎
12. 魚片
13. 特價
14. 原價
15. 炸
16. 煮
17. 對身體好

a. 炸鸡
b. 特价
c. 止
d. 可以
e. 煎
f. 至
g. 鸡丁
h. 煮
i. 炒
j. 对身体好
k. 原价
l. 蒸
m. 炸
n. 全鱼
o. 肉片
p. 鱼片
q. 肉丝

6. Practice writing.

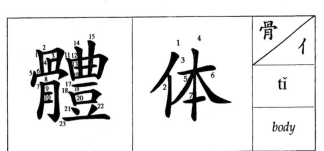

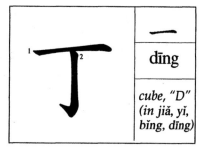

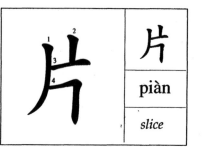

7. You are going to a Chinese friend's house for dinner tomorrow night. He leaves you the following note. Read it, and then write a brief (courteous) response.

你喜歡吃炸的還是炒的？能
吃魚嗎？肉呢？豆腐對身體
好，想嘗嘗嗎？還有，你愛
吃米飯還是麵條？

SEGMENT C: Specifying dishes.

1. Match the English and the Chinese names of the dishes below by writing the appropriate numbers in the circles.

STEAMED FISH 1. 餃子

DEEP FRIED CHICKEN 2. 炸雞

CHICKEN WITH GINGER & GREEN ONION 3. 什錦麵

RED-COOKED BEEF 4. 木須肉

SWEET SOUR PORK 5. 清蒸魚

CREPES WITH MEAT & VEGETABLE FILLING ④ 6. 薑蔥雞

PEKING DUCK 7. 糖醋肉

MEAT DUMPLINGS 8. 鍋巴湯

PORK SLIVERS W/MIXED VEGETABLES 9. 餛飩湯

NOODLES WITH MEAT & VEGETABLES 10. 酸辣湯

SIZZLING RICE SOUP ⑧ 11. 北京烤鴨

WONTON SOUP 12. 紅燒牛肉

HOT-SOUR SOUP 13. 肉絲什錦菜

2. You have been told to find out which of the following dishes are available at the Haohao Restaurant (menu on facing page). Check off the items available.

清蒸全魚 ☐   餃子 ☐

炸雞 ☐   肉絲什錦菜 ☐

薑蔥雞 ☐   什錦麵 ☐

紅燒牛肉 ☐   鍋巴湯 ☐

糖醋肉 ☐   餛飩湯 ☐

木須肉 ☐   酸辣湯 ☐

北京烤鴨 ☐

How many of each of the following are offered in this restaurant?

√soups ——————————————

√chicken dishes ——————   √duck dishes ——————————

√beef dishes ——————————   √pork dishes ——————————

√seafood dishes ——————   √shrimp dishes (under seafood) ————

√egg dishes ——————————   √vegetable dishes ——————

√fried rice dishes ——————   √fried noodle dishes ——————

√soup noodle dishes ————   √desserts ——————————

How much is the egg flower soup dish?

Shark's fin soup with crab meat is the most expensive soup. How much is it?

Bird's nest soup is another rare dish. How much is it?

When ordering for a group of people, a good guide is "one dish per person, plus soup (optional) and rice or noodles." If you had $60 to feed four people, what would you order from this menu? List below in English, with prices.

Number	Item	Price

湯類

酸辣湯 7.50

鍋巴湯 7.00

蛋花湯 6.50

燕窩湯 14.50

蟹肉魚翅湯 25.00

雞類

四川雞 9.50

宮保雞丁 9.50

油淋雞 11.50

腰果雞丁 8.50

糖醋雞 8.50

富貴雞 12.75

鴨類

北京鴨 35.00

香蘇鴨 19.50

燒鴨 12.75

海鮮類

糟溜魚片 11.50

甜酸魚球 10.50

蝦仁鍋巴 10.50

乾燒蝦球 11.25

蘭豆蝦球 9.50

清蒸全魚 15.75

牛肉類

青椒牛肉絲 ... 8.50

蒙古牛肉 8.70

芥蘭牛肉 8.90

蘭豆牛肉 8.50

蕃茄牛肉 8.25

豬肉類

木須肉 9.25

回鍋肉 7.50

糖醋肉 8.25

蛋類

蟹肉芙蛋 9.75

蝦仁芙蛋 8.25

素菜類

魚香茄子 7.50

羅漢齋 7.50

冬菇菜心 7.95

素什錦 7.75

麻婆豆腐 8.25

腐乳菠菜 6.50

飯類

叉燒炒飯 7.50

揚州炒飯 7.70

好好小館

炒麵

肉絲炒麵 9.50

海鮮麵 9.75

上海炒麵 8.50

星洲炒米粉 ... 9.20

湯麵

淨麵 4.00

海鮮湯麵 10.50

甜品

杏仁豆腐 2.50

3. Read aloud with a partner.

Situation 1

Two roommates are eating out.

甲： 你來點一個菜吧。   Come, you order a dish.

乙： 我不會。你點吧。   I don't know how. You order.

甲： 那你得告訴我你愛吃甚麼…   Then you have to tell me what you like to eat...

乙： 有烤鴨嗎？   Is there roast duck?

甲： 這兒沒有。你還愛吃甚麼？   They don't have it here. What else do you like to eat?

乙： 有紅燒牛肉嗎？   Is there red-cooked beef?

甲： 我看看…也沒有。那麼…   Let me see...there isn't. In that case...

乙： 我不是說我不會叫菜嗎？   Didn't I tell you I didn't know how to order? You order!
　　 你點吧！

甲： 那麼，吃餃子好不好？   Then, how about having *jiaozi?*

乙： 行，行，甚麼都行。   Fine, fine, anything will do. Just as long as it's quick. I'm starving to death.
　　 只要快，餓死我了！

Situation 2

A husband and wife are eating out.

男： 想喝湯嗎？   Would you like soup?

女： 喝也行不喝也行。   Either way is fine. (Having soup is fine, not having soup is also fine.)

男： 那就喝吧。甚麼湯？   Then's let's have some. What soup?

女： 酸辣湯。   Hot and sour soup.

男： 眞難喝！又酸又辣！   That tastes terrible! Both hot and sour!

女： 我就是喜歡酸辣呀。   That's just what I like, hot and sour.

男： 你喝吧，我不喝。   You have it. I won't have any.

女：　我一個人怎麼能喝那麼多？

　　　換一個湯吧，你要甚麼湯？

男：　鍋巴湯。

女：　我不愛吃鍋巴。肉絲湯呢？

男：　肉絲湯裡青菜不夠。

　　　豆腐湯好不好？

女：　這兒沒有豆腐湯啊！

男：　算了，別喝湯了。

How can I drink that much soup by myself? Or else let's change the soup. What soup do you want?

Sizzling rice soup.

I don't like sizzling rice. How about meat sliver soup?

There aren't enough vegetables in meat sliver soup. How would tofu soup be?

They don't have any tofu soup here!

Forget it. Let's not have soup.

4. Summary. For each word in English below, fill in the *pinyin* , the corresponding number for traditional characters and the corresponding letter for simplified characters.

sweet sour			
gyoza, dumplings			
wonton, dumplings			
hot and sour			
sweet	*tián*		
chicken category			
soup category	*tāng lèi*		
to order a dish			
to tell	*gàosu*		
as long as	*zhǐyào*		
be starving to death	*è sǐ le*		
not enough	*bú gòu*		
Forget it. Never mind.	*suàn le*		
don't			

1. 告訴   a. 只要
2. 餛飩   b. 饺子
3. 雞類   c. 点菜
4. 只要   d. 糖醋
5. 糖醋   e. 算了
6. 甜   f. 不够
7. 點菜   g. 馄饨
8. 別   h. 甜
9. 算了   i. 告诉
10. 餓死了   j. 汤类
11. 餃子   k. 酸辣
12. 不夠   l. 鸡类
13. 湯類   m. 饿死了
14. 酸辣   n. 別

5. Practice writing.

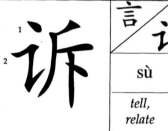

口
gào
tell, inform

言／讠
sù
tell, relate

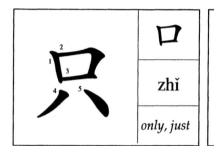

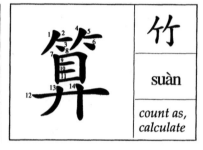

口
zhǐ
only, just

刀
bié
don't

竹
suàn
count as, calculate

歹
sǐ
die

6. A friend with whom you will be dining tomorrow night at your favorite restaurant, the Beijing Lou (544-8002), leaves you the following note.

我去订北京烤鸭。请告诉
我北京楼的电话号码。

(订 dìng means to order in advance.) Respond with the information sought. Ask your friend to tell you how much the duck will cost. Ask him/her not to order the duck if it is too expensive.

SEGMENT D: Requesting drinks and other menu items.

1. The canopy of this coffee-house in Taipei advertises the following items (not in order).

Western refreshments ☐

coffee ☐

fast food ☐

bread ☐

Number these items in the order in which they appear on the canopy.

2. Below right are a set of discount coupons for a McDonald's Restaurant in Taipei, valid from

_____ to _____, 19_____ . (Remember the year 1911).

    Fill in the blanks in the chart below.

PRICE	SANDWICH	DRINK	SIDE ORDER
$85		*Small corn chowder*	*Medium fries*
$83			
$69	*Cheeseburger*		*Apple pie*

3. On the following two pages are two sides of a breakfast menu from a PRC hotel for foreigners . Circle the Chinese characters for the English terms listed on the right-side page, then fill in their *pinyin* equivalents in the spaces on the left.

早 餐 預 定 表

1. —— ——

2. —— ——

房间编号	賓客姓名
日期	签署

3. —— ——

选择早餐时间

☐6:30～7:00　☐7:00～7:30　☐7:30～8:00　☐8:00～8:30
　　　　　　　☐8:30～9:00　☐9:00～9:30　☐9:30～10:00

4. —— ——

5. —— ——

人数	美国式早餐

・汁类
☐桔子水　☐胡罗卜汁　☐西柚汁
・麦片
☐麦片粥
・鲜蛋
☐搅　☐煎　☐煮（　）分钟
配
☐火腿　☐肠　☐咸肉
☐蛋卷　配
☐蘑菇　☐火腿　☐洋葱　☐忌司
・面包
☐丹麦包　☐羊角酥　☐土司
・牛油、果酱、蜂蜜
・水果
☐季节水果　☐水果杯
・饮料
☐咖啡　☐英国茶　☐中国茶

￥28.00

6. ——

7. ——

8. ——

9.

10. *miàn bāo*

11. *niú yóu*

12. —— ——

13. —— —— ——

14. —— ——

15. —— ——

16. —— ——

17. —— —— ——

人数	欧陆式早餐

・汁类
☐桔子水　☐蕃茄汁　☐西柚汁
・面包
☐丹麦包　☐羊角酥　☐土司
・牛油、果酱、蜂蜜
・水果
☐季节水果　☐水果杯
・饮料
☐咖啡　☐英国茶　☐中国茶

￥25.00

18. *guǒ jiàng*

BREAKFAST ORDER SHEET

1. breakfast
   (2 characters)

ROOM NO.	NAME PLEASE PRINT
DATE	SIGNATURE

2. room (2)

Time required (Please indicate)

3. time (2)

☐6:30–7:00　　☐7:00–7:30　☐7:30–8:00　☐8:00–8:30
　　　　　　　☐8:30–9:00　☐9:00–9:30　☐9:30–10:00

PERSONS	AMERICAN BREAKFAST

4. # of persons (2)
5. American style (3)

• Juice
☐Orange　☐Tomato　☐Grapefruit

6. juices (1)

• Cereals
☐Porridge
• Two Eggs

7. egg (1)

☐Scrambled　☐Fried　☐Boiled(　)mts.

8. fried (1)

served with

9. boiled (1)

☐Ham　☐Sausage　☐Bacon
☐Omelette served with
☐Mushroom　☐Ham　☐Onion　☐Cheese
• Bread

10. bread (2)

☐Danish Pastry　☐Croissant　☐Toast

11. butter (2)

• Butter, Jam, Honey
• Fruit
☐Fresh Fruit in Season　☐Fruit Cup

12. fruit (2)
13. fruit cup (3)

• Beverage

14. drinks (2)

☐Coffee　☐English tea

15. coffee (2)

☐Chinese Tea

16. English tea (3)

¥ 28.00

17. Chinese tea (3)

PERSONS	CONTINENTAL BREAKFAST

• Juice
☐Orange　☐Tomato　Grapefruit
• Bread
☐Danish Pastry　☐Croissant　☐Toast

18. jam (2)

• Butter, Jam, Honey
• Fruit
☐Fresh Fruit in Season　☐Fruit Cup
• Beverage
☐Coffee　☐Decaffeinated Coffee　☐English Tea
☐Chinese Tea

¥ 25.00

4. You will be going grocery shopping soon, and receive the following requests from your roommates, one of whom is from the PRC and the other from Hong Kong. What are you to buy for them? Fill in the blanks in the list provided.

小王

　　請幫我買一大箱可樂
和一瓶牛奶。

　　　　　　林
　　　　　94.5-17

小王：

　　請幫我買六桶果汁和一瓶
白酒。

　　　　　　　故 94.5.17

√6 cans _____

√1 bottle _____

√1 bottle _____

√1 case _____

5. Read aloud with a partner.

<u>Situation 1</u>

A thirsty customer sits down in a restaurant.

客人：	有甚麼飲料？	What drinks are there?
服務員：	有茶、咖啡、啤酒、汽水、果汁。	There's tea, coffee, beer, soda, juice.
客人：	有牛奶嗎？	Do you have milk?
服務員：	對不起，沒有。	Sorry, we don't.
客人：	請給我一瓶汽水。	Please give me a bottle of soda.
服務員：	好的。	Alright.
客人：	要冰的。	I'd like it cold (iced).
服務員：	行。	Fine.

Situation 2

A husband and wife are eating out.

先生：菜單給我們了沒有？

Have they given us the menus yet?

太太：還沒有。餐具餐巾也沒拿來。

Not yet. They haven't brought utensils or napkins either.

先生：真是太慢了。

They really are too slow.

服務員：你們需要甚麼？

What do you folks need?

太太：我們甚麼都需要，

　　　請先把菜單拿來。

We need everything. Please bring the menus first.

Situation 3

A father is charged with preparing the next day's breakfast.

爸爸：小真，你明天早餐想吃甚麼？

Xiao Zhen, what do you want for breakfast tomorrow?

小真：兩片麵包，兩個雞蛋，

　　　牛奶和水果。

Two slices of bread, two eggs, milk and fruit.

爸爸：你能吃那麼多啊！

You can eat that much!

小真：能，我每天都吃那麼多。

I can. I eat that much every day.

Situation 4

Two Chinese friends are chatting.

甲：你愛吃西餐嗎？

Do you like Western food?

乙：有的我愛吃。有些飲料我也愛

　　喝，像 (xiàng) 可樂啊，果汁啊…

I like some (of it). I also like some Western (soft) drinks, such as cola, or juice, or...

甲：你愛喝奶茶嗎？

Do you like tea with milk?

乙：不行，我喝咖啡可以加牛奶，

　　可是茶不能加奶，我還是

　　中國人啊！

No way. When I drink coffee I can add milk, but I can't add milk to tea. I'm still Chinese!

6. Summary. For each word in English below, fill in the *pinyin*, the corresponding number for traditional characters and the corresponding letter for simplified characters.

fast food			
coffee			
bread			
hamburger	*hànbǎo*		
small (cup of) tea	*xiǎo bēi chá*		
french fries	*shǔtiáo*		
medium soda			
apple pie	*píngguǒ pài*		
American-style	*Měiguó shì*		
fruit juice			
butter	*niúyóu*		
fruit	*shuǐguǒ*		
soft drinks	*yǐnliào*		
cola			
milk			
slice			
beer			
bottle			
ice, icy			
menu			
eating utensils	*cānjù*		
napkin	*cānjīn*		
to bring			
to need	*xūyào*		
both... and...	*yòu...yòu...*		

1.	冰	a.	快餐
2.	漢堡	b.	拿来
3.	餐巾	c.	牛油
4.	牛油	d.	瓶
5.	快餐	e.	菜单
6.	美國式	f.	水果
7.	可樂	g.	小杯茶
8.	拿來	h.	汉堡
9.	中杯汽水	i.	餐具
10.	片	j.	啤酒
11.	水果	k.	果汁
12.	又…又…	l.	饮料
13.	咖啡	m.	可乐
14.	菜單	n.	面包
15.	啤酒	o.	苹果派
16.	小杯茶	p.	冰
17.	需要	q.	又…又…
18.	飲料	r.	中杯汽水
19.	餐具	s.	需要
20.	薯條	t.	美国式
21.	牛奶	u.	咖啡
22.	果汁	v.	餐巾
23.	麵包	w.	牛奶
24.	蘋果派	x.	片
25.	瓶	y.	薯条

7. You will be teaching English in a remote city in the PRC. Your predecessor, a European, has left you some notes to help you adjust to life in this city, including the following comments. Based on these comments, predict how often you'll be able to enjoy the drinks listed by checking the appropriate box.

—茶又好，又便宜。

—牛奶要天天喝，也不太貴。

—可口可乐不错，可是很貴。

　不能常常喝。

—咖啡买不到。

—啤酒好喝，可是太貴了。

　也不能常喝。

—果汁买不到。

	often	seldom	never
beer			
milk			
juice			
tea			
coffee			
Coca-cola			

8. Practice writing.

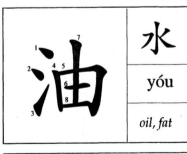

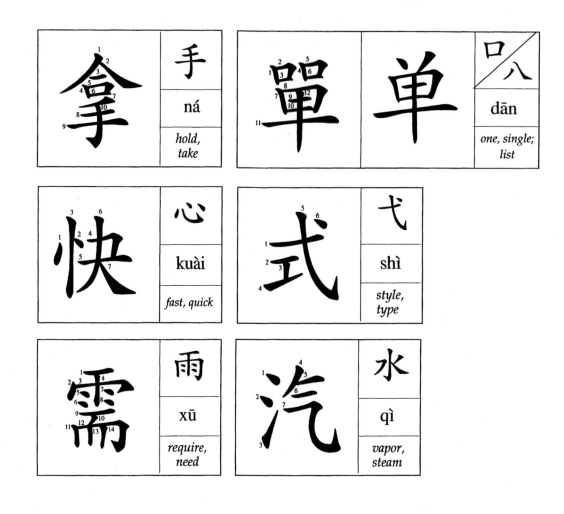

7. A friend is making a trip into town and has offered to pick up anything you need from a market or restaurant. Write a note asking him/her to buy you five food or drink items (of your choice).

SEGMENT A: Specifying establishments in town.

1. This is the entryway to a large outdoor market in a provincial town in the PRC.

Which way does the sign read? Check one.

➡

⬅

The last two characters in the sign say "market." Circle and label these.

2. Circle and label the following terms in the two signs below, one advertising a souvenir shop and the other a hotel.

travel (lǚyóu)

souvenir (jìniànpǐn)

store, shop (shāngdiàn)

hotel (lǚguǎn)

3. The pictures on these two pages are of a number of public and commercial establishments in the PRC and Taiwan. Match the English to their names by writing the appropriate numbers in the boxes below (which represent the pictures).

1. Hospital
2. Xinjian Hotel
3. Campus Book House
4. Bank of Taiwan
5. West Lake Park
6. Zhongxiao Produce Market
7. School
8. Restaurant

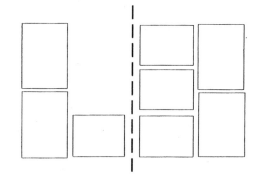

4. What is this place? Check one.

     a school   ☐

     a movie theatre   ☐

     a clinic   ☐

     a store   ☐

Circle and label when the event advertised starts.

Circle and label the term "ticket price."

What is the large-character text in the middle? Check one.

     name of a person   ☐

     brand name of a product   ☐

     title of a lecture   ☐

     title of a film   ☐

5. This is a bus stop sign in Beijing. Circle and label the following items.

     number of the route

     time of the earliest bus

     time of the latest bus

     the term "public bus"

Which of the following is a bus stop on this route? Check off.

     People's University   ☐

     Qinghua University   ☐

     Heping Avenue South   ☐

     Heping Avenue North   ☐

     Ox-king Temple   ☐

Write the name of the current stop in *pinyin*._____
It means "Outside (the) De(sheng Gate) (of the old walled city)."

6. You are holding this ticket to a show at the 2-7 Playhouse. Where is your seat?

upstairs ☐

downstairs ☐

row # _____

seat # _____

7. This stub is for the Southeast Asian Grand Theater. Circle and label the theater's name.

The ticket is (check one)

full price ☐

half price ☐

complimentary ☐

8. Below are two photographs. Study the one on the left, and then indicate what the sign on the right says. (Check one.)

Dali City ☐

tour office ☐

ticket counter ☐

9. This pamphlet is distributed by the Childhood Burn Foundation of The Republic of China on Taiwan. According to these instructions, in what order should the following actions be taken, in case a severe burn occurs? Number as appropriate.

SEND to the hospital. ☐

REMOVE clothing under water. ☐

DOUSE with cold water. [1]

COVER with a towel. ☐

SOAK in cold water. ☐

10. Read aloud with a partner.

Situation 1

A doctor is about to leave the hospital.

服務員：　王醫生，您上哪兒去？　　Where are you going, Dr. Wang?

醫生：　　到飛機場去接人。　　　　To the airport to pick someone up.

服務員：　接誰？　　　　　　　　　Who are you picking up?

醫生：　　接來我們醫院工作
　　　　　的一個人。　　　　　　　Someone who will be working in our hospital.

Situation 2

A mother and daughter are preparing to go out.

媽媽：走吧。　　　　　　　　　　Let's go.

小眞：到哪兒去？　　　　　　　　Where are we going?

媽媽：去看電影啊。　　　　　　　To the movies (of course).

小眞：爲甚麼要這麼早去？　　　Why do we have to go so early?

媽媽：我們得先去加油站加油。　We have to go to the gas-station to get gas first.

小眞：可是姐姐還沒回家呢。　　But elder sister's not home yet.

媽媽：姐姐在電影院門前等我們。Sister will wait for us in front of the movie theatre.

小眞：姐姐怎麼去電影院？　　　How will she get to the theatre?

媽媽：她自己開車。　　　　　　She'll drive herself.

小眞：開誰的汽車呢？　　　　　Who's car will she drive?

媽媽：王阿姨的。別多説了，走吧。Aunty Wang's. Enough, let's go.

小眞：那王阿姨開甚麼呢？　　　Then what will Aunty Wang drive?

媽媽：她坐公共汽車。　　　　　She'll take the bus.

小眞：王阿姨爲甚麼要去坐
　　　公共汽車？　　　　　　Why does Aunty Wang want to take the bus?

媽媽：因爲她把汽車借給姐姐了。Because she loaned her car to your sister. Go, go, go, stop asking and asking questions.
　　　走走走，別老問個不停。

Situation 3

On a street in a Chinese city, a visitor asks two students, one Chinese and one foreign, for directions.

甲：請問，遠東飯店在哪兒？　May I ask where the *Yuandong Fandian* is?

乙：對不起，我不知道。　　　I'm sorry, I don't know.

丙：遠東飯店是甚麼？是飯館嗎？What is the *Yuandong Fandian*? Is it a restaurant?

甲：不，是旅館。　　　　　　No, it's a hotel.

丙：噢，那我知道，在郵局對面有
　　　一家旅館。　　　　　　Oh, then I know. There's a hotel across from the post office.

甲：哪裡？　　　　　　　　　Where?

丙：　在郵局對面，警察局的旁邊，
　　　在圖書館那兒。

Across from the post office, next to the police station, near the library.

甲：　遠嗎？

Is it far?

丙：　不遠。半里路就到了。

It's not far. A half mile and you're there.

甲：　那是很近。謝謝你了。

That is close. Thank you then.

丙：　不要客氣。

You're welcome.

　　　（甲走了）

(Jia leaves.)

丙：　為甚麼把旅館叫飯店？

Why do they call a hotel a *fandian* (restaurant)?

乙：　大旅館都叫飯店。

Big hotels are called *fandian*.

Situation 4

Two brothers are at home together.

哥哥：南海市場離書店遠嗎？

Is the South Seas Market far from the bookstore?

弟弟：甚麼書店？

What bookstore?

哥哥：中華書店。

China Books.

弟弟：哪兒有個中華書店？

Where is there a China Books?

哥哥：美國銀行跟圖書館中間
　　　不是有個中華書店嗎？

Isn't there a China Books between the Bank of America and the library?

弟弟：我忘了。

I forget.

哥哥：嘿，你這個人真是⋯
　　　一點兒用都沒有。

Hah, you are such a...you're no use at all.

11. Summary. For each word in English below, fill in the *pinyin*, the corresponding number for traditional characters and the corresponding letter for simplified characters.

English	pinyin	#	letter
market			
to travel, tour	*lǔyóu*		
store, shop	*shāngdiàn*		
hotel			
bookstore			
hospital			
restaurant			
public park			
bank			
public bus			
Peace Avenue	*Hépíng Jiē*		
ticket counter/window	*shòupiàochù*		
...row...seat	*...pái...hào*		
theater, playhouse	*jùchǎng*		
theater, playhouse	*xìyuàn*		
send to the hospital	*sòng yīyuàn*		
pick up an arrival	*jiē rén*		
airport			
gas station			
movie theater			
oneself	*zìjǐ*		
drive a car			
far from here	*lí zhèr yuǎn*		
near here			
useless	*méiyòng*		

1. 飛機場　　a. 接人
2. 醫院　　　b. 送医院
3. 戲院　　　c. …排…号
4. 自己　　　d. 售票处
5. 旅遊　　　e. 和平街
6. 離這兒遠　f. 商店
7. …排…號　g. 医院
8. 書店　　　h. 没用
9. 接人　　　i. 加油站
10. 公園　　　j. 饭馆
11. 沒用　　　k. 飞机场
12. 和平街　　l. 市场
13. 電影院　　m. 银行
14. 商店　　　n. 书店
15. 開汽車　　o. 公共汽车
16. 飯館　　　p. 自己
17. 加油站　　q. 剧场
18. 銀行　　　r. 旅馆
19. 劇場　　　s. 离这儿远
20. 售票處　　t. 离这儿近
21. 旅館　　　u. 电影院
22. 送醫院　　v. 戏院
23. 市場　　　w. 公园
24. 離這兒近　x. 开汽车
25. 公共汽車　y. 旅游

12. Practice writing.

巾 shì market, city	場	場	土 chǎng gathering place, stage
車	车	車/车 chē vehicle	票	示 piào ticket
送	辶 sòng give as a gift, see off	近	辶 jìn near	商	口 shāng business, trade
接	手 jiē receive, meet, welcome	自	自 zì self, from/ since	己	己 jǐ oneself
離	离	隹/二 lí leave; away from	遠	远	辶 yuǎn far, distant

13. Leave a note for your roommate saying you are going out. Name some places you will be stopping by, and say when you'll be back.

SEGMENT B: Specifying points beyond the community.

1. Write the *pinyin* equivalents of the terms below.

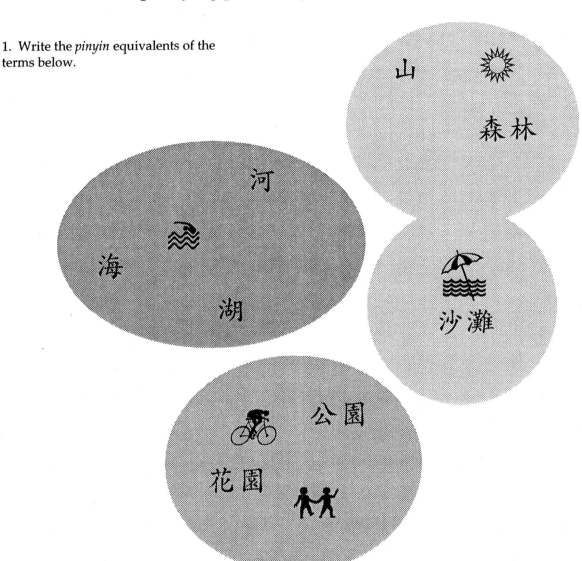

2. Read aloud with a partner.

<u>Situation 1</u>

Two students who share an apartment meet at their door.

甲：上哪兒去？　　　　　　Where are you going?

乙：到河邊玩去。　　　　　To the riverside, to relax.

甲：跟誰一塊兒？　　　　　Who are you going with?

乙：一個外國朋友。　　　　A friend from a foreign country.

Situation 2

Zhang and Li are co-workers. Li has been away on vacation.

張：	小李你回來了。	Li, you're back.
李：	嗯。	Uh-huh.
張：	甚麼時候回來的？	When did you get back?
李：	昨天晚上。	Yesterday evening.
張：	到哪些地方去玩了？	Which places did you go (on your trip)?
李：	到海邊兒玩了兩天，山上玩了兩天。	We went to the seaside for a couple of days, and to the mountains for a couple of days.
張：	山上有甚麼好玩的？	What is there to do in the mountains?
李：	到山上的森林裡走走真有意思。	It's really interesting to walk in the forests in the mountains.
張：	就是，希望我下個月也能有空出去走一走。你玩得好嗎？	That's right, I hope I'll have the time next month to get out a bit too. Did you have fun?
李：	很好，你也應該去一去。	Lots. You should go too.

Situation 3

A, a Chinese-American living in Hawaii, is visiting his relative B, who lives in Hong Kong.

甲：	你們到了週末喜歡做甚麼？	What do you like to do on weekends?
乙：	我們住在城裡有好多可以做的，我最喜歡到街上去走。	Since we live in the city there is a lot to do. I most enjoy just walking around on the streets.
甲：	你們街上老是人山人海，有甚麼好走的？我喜歡到沙灘上去睡覺。	Your streets are so crowded (filled with mountains and oceans of people), how can you walk around? I like to sleep on the beach.
乙：	沙灘上人也是很多，又那麼熱，有甚麼好玩的？	There are lots of people on the beach too, and it's so hot. What's the fun in that?

3. Summary. For each word in English below, fill in the *pinyin*, the corresponding number for traditional characters, and the corresponding letter for simplified characters.

English	pinyin		
mountain			
forest			
beach			
river			
lake			
ocean			
public park			
flower garden			
relax, have fun			
uh-huh (grunt of agreement)	ng		
be interesting			
be fun; cute	hǎowán		
that's right; just so	jiù shì		
hope	xīwàng		
ought to	yīnggāi		
weekend	zhōumò		
downtown, in town			
always, all the time	lǎoshì		
be very crowded	rénshān-rénhǎi		

1. 河
2. 公園
3. 有意思
4. 海
5. 老是
6. 玩
7. 城裡
8. 森林
9. 希望
10. 就是
11. 沙灘
12. 應該
13. 花園
14. 嗯
15. 人山人海
16. 山
17. 週末
18. 湖
19. 好玩

a. 人山人海
b. 老是
c. 应该
d. 城里
e. 希望
f. 花园
g. 有意思
h. 山
i. 就是
j. 湖
k. 河
l. 嗯
m. 周末
n. 沙滩
o. 海
p. 好玩
q. 森林
r. 玩
s. 公园

4. Practice writing.

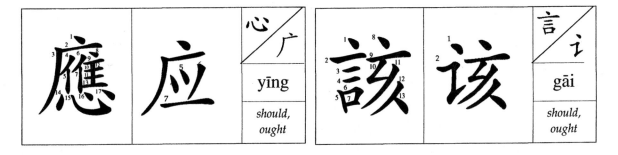

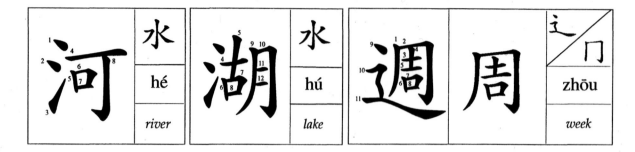

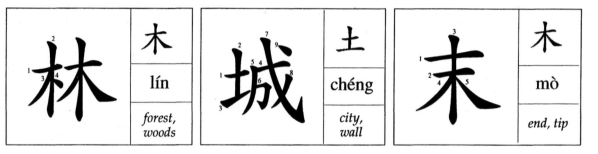

5. You receive this note from two of your classmates.

我們想這個週末到山上或海邊去玩。你有時間一起去嗎？

Write a response saying you'd like to join them. Make one or two suggestions about where you could go together.

SEGMENT C: Directions around town.

1. Label the captions according to the photographs.

    a. YIELD   b. Incoming traffic from the right   c. Cars forbidden to enter

    d. STOP   e. Stop the vehicle, then proceed   f. Major road ahead

2. Match the English and the Chinese captions provided below to the appropriate photograph.

⌐ ┬ ┐
└ ┴ ┘

⌐ ┬ ┐
├ ┼ ┤
└ ┴ ┘

⌐ ┬ ┐
└ ┴ ┘

甲. 高速公路

乙. 停車場入口

丙. 行人請走
　　地下道

丁. 繳費進場

3. Match the captions to the photographs.

A. No stopping 8 a.m. to noon, 3 p.m. to 8 p.m.
B. SLOW
C. One-way street
D. Please pay attention to traffic safety
E. Drive slowly
F. Public safety bureau ordinance

4. Read aloud with a partner.

Situation 1

Li seeks directions of A, a passerby on the street in Beijing.

李：請問，到火車站怎麼走？　　　　　　May I ask the way to the train station?

甲：這條路一直走，到紅綠燈那　　　　　Go straight on this road, turn right at the
　　　　　　　　　　　　　　　　　　　light, and the station is on the left hand side
　　兒往右拐，車站就在馬路左邊。　　　of the street..

李：謝謝了。　　　　　　　　　　　　　Thank you, then.

Situation 2

Wang seeks directions of A.

王：百貨大樓在哪個方向，您知道嗎？　　Which direction is the shopping arcade, do
　　　　　　　　　　　　　　　　　　　you know?

甲：甚麼？百貨大樓？我不知道。　　　　What? Shopping arcade? I don't know.

He tries again with B and C, who are walking together.

王：您知道百貨大樓在哪兒嗎？　　　　　Do you know where the shopping arcade is?

乙：這兒沒有百貨大樓啊…　　　　　　　There's no shopping arcade here...

丙：有，有，就在那邊兒。　　　　　　　There is. There is. It's right over there.

王：怎麼走啊？　　　　　　　　　　　　How do I get there?

丙：一直走，走到中國銀行那兒向左　　　Go straight. When you get to the Bank of
　　　　　　　　　　　　　　　　　　　China, turn left, the shopping arcade is
　　轉，百貨大樓就在中國銀行後頭。　　behind the Bank of China.

乙：不對。銀行後頭是京都飯店。　　　　That's not right. Behind the bank is the
　　　　　　　　　　　　　　　　　　　Capitol (Jīngdū) Hotel.

丙：是啊。要經過京都飯店。再過去　　　That's right. You have to pass by the
　　　　　　　　　　　　　　　　　　　Capitol Hotel. Just a little past it is the
　　一點就是百貨大樓啊。　　　　　　　shopping arcade.

乙：是嗎？我還不知道呢。　　　　　　　Is that so? I didn't even know.

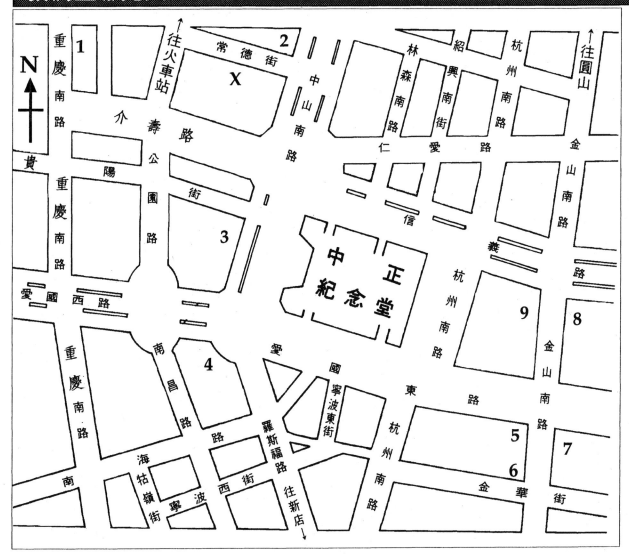

5. This is the downtown area of Taipei.　The complex in the center of the map is the Chiang Kaishek Memorial Hall（中正紀念堂）. You are staying at the YMCA, marked by the X.　Read the Chinese descriptions, then identify each of the locations marked by the numbers 1–9.

對面有一個大飯店。

到常德街向左轉，到了公園路再左轉，走到介壽街向右轉。在第二個路口向右轉。在右邊有書店。

金山南路有一家很好的飯館，在愛國東路和信義路中間，路的西邊。

飯館對面是一個電影院。

中山南路有一個很大的圖書館，在中正紀念堂對面，學校的北邊。

愛國東路跟金山南路的路口那兒有一個加油站，在郵局對面。郵局旁邊是銀行。

1. _____

2. _____

3. _____

4. _____

5. *Post office*　（郵局）
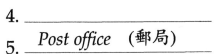

6. _____

7. _____

8. _____

9. _____

6. Summary.

YIELD	*ràng*		
STOP	*tíng*		
forbidden, prohibited	*jìnzhǐ*		
enter			
right side	*yòu cè*		
freeway, highway			
parking lot	*tíngchēchǎng*		
entrance			
pedestrian			
underground passage			
go straight ahead			
turn	*zhuǎn/guǎi*		
traffic light			
shopping building/ arcade			
East Patriotism Road			
know			
pass by			
intersection			
Memorial Hall	*Jìniàntáng*		
direction	*fāngxiàng*		
one way street	*dānxíngdào*		
to notice, pay attention to	*zhùyì*		
traffic	*jiāotōng*		
safety	*ānquán*		
slow	*màn*		
Public Security Bureau	*gōngānjú*		

1. 禁止　　　a. 进入
2. 經過　　　b. 注意
3. 單行道　　c. 知道
4. 地下道　　d. 停
5. 愛國東路　e. 百货大楼
6. 安全　　　f. 右侧
7. 轉／拐　　g. 直走
8. 知道　　　h. 公安局
9. 右側　　　i. 经过
10. 方向　　　j. 高速公路
11. 注意　　　k. 慢
12. 停　　　　l. 让
13. 紀念堂　　m. 方向
14. 直走　　　n. 禁止
15. 公安局　　o. 行人
16. 百貨大樓　p. 转／拐
17. 行人　　　q. 爱国东路
18. 進入　　　r. 停车场
19. 路口　　　s. 红绿灯
20. 停車場　　t. 入口
21. 交通　　　u. 纪念堂
22. 高速公路　v. 单行道
23. 讓　　　　w. 路口
24. 慢　　　　x. 地下道
25. 入口　　　y. 安全
26. 紅綠燈　　z. 交通

7. Practice writing.

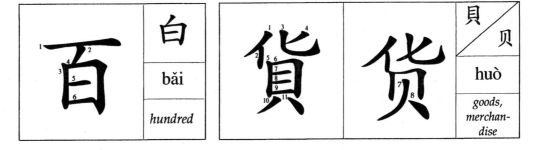

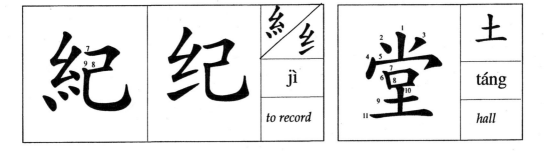

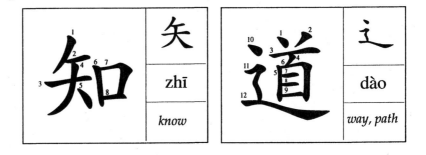

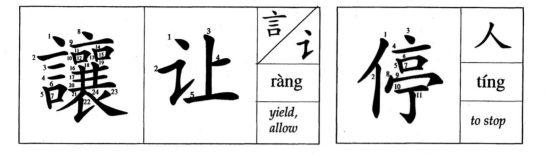

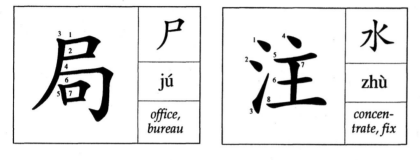

讓	让	言 / 讠
		ràng
		yield, allow

停	人
	tíng
	to stop

局	尸
	jú
	office, bureau

注	水
	zhù
	concentrate, fix

安	宀
	ān
	calm, safe

全	入
	quán
	whole, entire

8. Write some brief directions to a Chinese friend, telling how to get from your school to your home.

_____

_____

_____

_____

_____

SEGMENT D: Points around the world; weather reports.

1. Label the place names on these three continents (not shown to scale or in their naturally occurring locations!) with English and *pinyin*.

北京　漢城　東京
西安
上海
桂林　廣州　臺北
香港

芝加哥　紐約
三藩市
華盛頓
洛杉磯

倫敦　柏林　巴黎
馬德里

2. What and where is this place?

_____

_____

NANFANG　RIBAO　　　第15872号

1993年 8月
21
星期六
农历癸酉年七月初四
处暑：农历七月初六
广州市区天气预报
阴间多云有暴雨
风向　东南
风力　6级阵风8级，转偏
　　　南风4级
温度　最高30°C
　　　最低24°C
相对湿度　70%～95%

3. Above is the banner head of a PRC newspaper. The box contains the weather report/forecast for the day.

• What day is it for?　　Year:_____ Month:_____ Day:_____

　　　　　　　　　　　Day of the week: _____

• 報紙 bàozhǐ means "newspaper." 報 by itself means "to report." What is an appropriate translation for *Nanfang Ribao*? _____

• "Weather forecast" is tiānqì yùbào. Circle and label this term.

• The weather forecast for the day is "Overcast, heavy cloud cover, occasional heavy rain." The *pinyin* equivalent is yīn jiān duō yún yǒu bàoyǔ. Circle and label the characters.

	wind direction	
	relative humidity	
	highest temperature	
• Fill in the following information.	lowest temperature	

4. Read aloud with a partner.

Situation 1

Two acquaintances are chatting.

張： 你去過歐洲嗎？

Have you been to Europe?

陳： 去過歐洲幾個地方。去過西班牙的馬德里，還有巴黎和倫敦。

I've been a few places in Europe. I've been to Madrid, Spain, and to Paris and London.

張： 那邊天氣怎麼樣？

How's the weather over there?

陳： 很難説，有時候冷，有時候熱。可是倫敦和巴黎冬天會比馬德里冷。

It's hard to say. Cold sometimes, hot at others. But in winter London and Paris are colder than Madrid.

Situation 2

Wang, a Chinese student in the US, and Li, her American friend, are looking ahead to their summer vacations.

王： 今年暑假到哪兒去玩嗎？

Are you going anywhere (on holiday) this summer vacation?

李： 我們去加州幾天，到三藩市和洛杉磯。

We're going to California for a few days, (visiting) San Francisco and Los Angeles.

王： 你們每年都去加州啊。

Oh, you go to California every year.

李： 對，因為我爸爸住在洛杉磯，我媽媽住在三藩市。我去看看他們。你呢？你去哪兒嗎？

Right, because my father lives in Los Angeles and my mother lives in San Francisco. I go to see them. How about you? Are you going anywhere?

王： 我七月回中國一次。

I'm taking a trip back to China in July.

李： 太好了！中國甚麼地方？

That's great! Where in China?

王： 我回上海一個月，去廣州兩天、桂林兩天。

I'm going back to Shanghai for a month, and then to Canton for two days and Guilin for two days.

李： 多好啊！

How wonderful!

5. Summary. For each word in English below, fill in the *pinyin* , the corresponding number for traditional characters and the corresponding letter for simplified characters.

English	pinyin		
Guilin			
Canton			
Taipei			
Hong Kong			
New York			
Chicago			
San Francisco	*Sānfānshì*		
Los Angeles			
Washington			
Tokyo			
Paris			
London			
Daily News			
weather forecast	*tiānqì yùbào*		
heavy cloud cover	*duō yún*		
torrential rain	*bào yǔ*		
temperature	*wēndù*		
hard to say			
every year	*měinián*		
once, one time, one occasion	*yí cì*		

1.　巴黎　　　　a.　芝加哥
2.　溫度　　　　b.　桂林
3.　紐約　　　　c.　三藩市
4.　暴雨　　　　d.　日报
5.　桂林　　　　e.　纽约
6.　華盛頓　　　f.　天气预报
7.　一次　　　　g.　香港
8.　三藩市　　　h.　台北
9.　倫敦　　　　i.　每年
10.　臺北　　　　j.　巴黎
11.　天氣預報　　k.　东京
12.　廣州　　　　l.　难说
13.　芝加哥　　　m.　华盛顿
14.　多雲　　　　n.　广州
15.　東京　　　　o.　一次
16.　香港　　　　p.　温度
17.　日報　　　　q.　洛杉矶
18.　每年　　　　r.　伦敦
19.　洛杉磯　　　s.　多云
20.　難説　　　　t　暴雨

6. Practice writing.

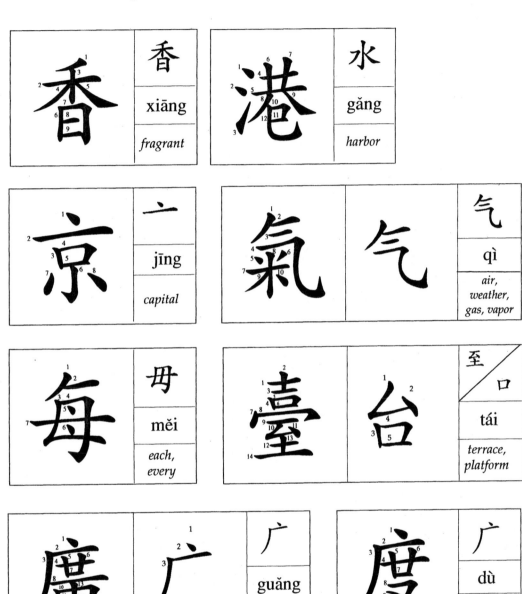

	香 xiāng *fragrant*		水 gǎng *harbor*
	亠 jīng *capital*		气 qì *air, weather, gas, vapor*
	毋 měi *each, every*		至 / 口 tái *terrace, platform*
	广 guǎng *wide, vast*		广 dù *degree (unit of measurement)*

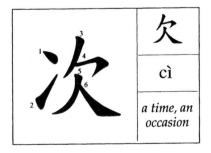

| | 欠
cì
a time, an occasion |

7. Pretend you live in Hawaii and receive the following note from a friend in Asia.
(廣告 guǎnggào = advertisement)

小王：

　　我昨天看到你們 Hawaii 的一張廣
告，那兒的天氣真的那麼好嗎？我們這兒天
氣報告老是『多雲暴雨』，真沒意思。

　　希望你給我回信。

黃

94.4.18

Write back, describe Hawaii's good weather, and invite your friend to visit.

小黃：

_____

_____

_____

_____

_____

_____

_____

SEGMENT E: Modes of transportation.

坐飛機

1. Label the Chinese terms in *pinyin*.

坐出租汽車 (PRC)

坐計程車 (Taiwan)

坐的士 (Hong Kong)

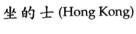

騎自行車

坐地鐵

坐火車

坐公共汽車

坐船

走路

2. The banner advertizes a roadside repair stall in the PRC.

•What does this stall repair most of all?

_____

•Hand-pushed carts and three-wheeled pedicabs can also be repaired here. Circle and label in English the characters for these terms.

•The sign also reads "fast repairs," "serving you," "satisfaction guaranteed," and "preferential prices." The first expression is two characters, the remainder are four. Circle and label in English the characters that match these expressions.

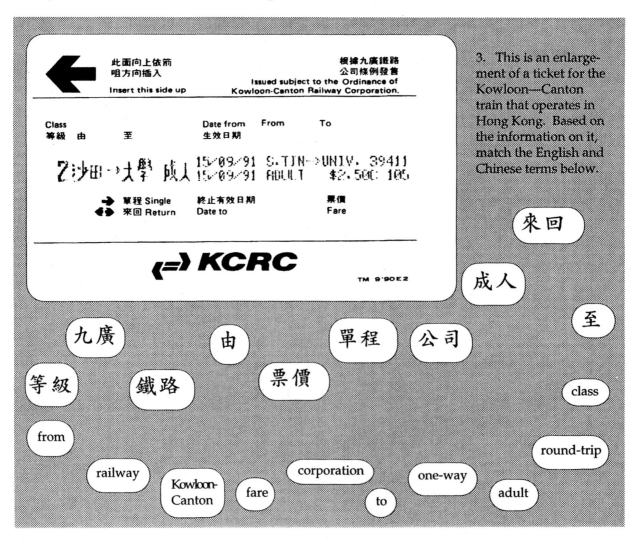

3. This is an enlargement of a ticket for the Kowloon—Canton train that operates in Hong Kong. Based on the information on it, match the English and Chinese terms below.

來回

成人

至

九廣   由   單程   公司

等級   鐵路   票價

class

from

round-trip

railway   Kowloon-Canton   fare   corporation   to   one-way   adult

4. Read aloud with a partner.

Situation 1

A is a Taiwanese student visiting his American friend B, who is studying in the PRC. They have been out sightseeing.

甲：　咱們叫個『的士』回去吧。

Let's get a "dīksí" back.

乙：　甚麼叫『dīksí』？

What is a "dīksí" ?

甲：　哈哈，就是出租汽車。我們臺灣叫計程車。『的士』是香港人的說法。

Ha ha. It's a taxicab. In Taiwan we call (taxis) "distance-recording cars." "Dīksí" is the way people in Hong Kong say it.

乙：　『dīksí』是甚麼字？

What characters are "dīksí"?

甲：　是『我的，你的』的『的』字，加上『女士』的『士』字。廣東人念『dīksí』，聽起來像英文的『taxi』。

They're the "de" of "wǒde, nǐde" plus the "shì" of "nǔshì." Cantonese read them as "dīksí," which sounds like the English "taxi."

乙：　是這樣，我懂了。可是我們還是走路回去吧，出租汽車太貴了。

So that's it. I understand. But we'd better walk back, after all. "Cars for hire" (taxis) are too expensive.

Situation 2

Two natives of Beijing and chatting with a woman from Hong Kong.

甲：香港有地鐵嗎？

Does Hong Kong have a subway?

乙：有啊，又快又好又便宜。

Yes! It's fast and good and inexpensive.

丙：北京也有，可是坐的人不太多。

Beijing has one too, but not too many people ride it.

乙：爲甚麼？

Why?

丙：自行車方便。

Bikes are more convenient.

甲：我不同意，我天天坐地鐵。

No, I don't agree. I take the subway every day.

5. Summary. For each word in English below, fill in the *pinyin*, the corresponding number for traditional characters, and the corresponding letter for simplified characters.

English	pinyin	#	letter
to walk			
to drive			
to ride a cab (PRC)			
to ride a cab (Taiwan)			
taxicab (Hong Kong)	dīshì		
to ride a train			
to ride a bus			
to take the subway			
to ride a bicycle			
to fly, take a plane			
to travel by ship			
"REPAIRS"	xiū		
"Serving you"	wèi nín fúwù		
one-way ticket	dānchéng piào		
round-trip ticket			
Kowloon—Canton	Jiǔlóng—Guǎngzhōu		
railway	tiělù		
class	děngjí		
adult	chéngrén		
company	gōngsī		
from(a place or time)	yóu		
to(a place or time)	zhì		
when one hears it	tīng qǐlái		
to agree	tóngyì		
every day			

1. 單程票   a. 骑自行车
2. 的士   b. 来回票
3. 等級   c. 同意
4. 爲您服務   d. 成人
5. 坐計程車   e. 坐出租汽车
6. 由   f. 坐飞机
7. 坐火車   g. 走路
8. 修   h. 坐公共汽车
9. 來回票   i. 坐地铁
10. 坐出租汽車   j. 等级
11. 坐船   k. 坐火车
12. 聽起來   l. 天天
13. 坐公共汽車   m. 听起来
14. 公司   n. 至
15. 九龍—廣州   o. 单程票
16. 開車   p. 为您服务
17. 至   q. 的士
18. 坐地鐵   r. 由
19. 坐飛機   s. 开车
20. 同意   t. 修
21. 鐵路   u. 坐船
22. 騎自行車   v. 九龙—广州
23. 成人   w. 坐计程车
24. 走路   x. 公司
25. 天天   y. 鐵路

6. Practice writing.

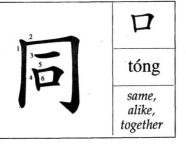

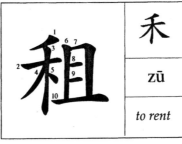

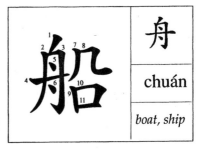

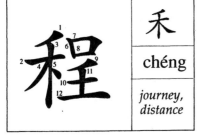

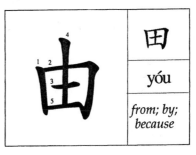

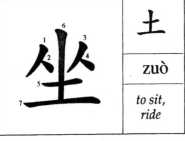

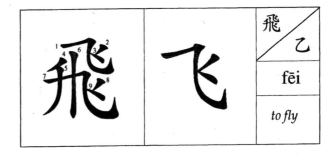

7. Your last name is Wang and you drive to school every day. Your friend Huang, who lives near your school, rides a bike to school. One day you receive the following note.

小王：

　　　我的自行車壞了，昨天去修理，明天才能好。你明天開車到學校來嗎？能不能接我一下？請今天晚上打電話告訴我。我的電話號碼是956-2692.

　　　多謝！

黃

94.4.18

You will be out tonight and cannot call. Write back instead. Say whether or not you can offer Huang a ride. If you cannot, give a reason. If you can, make arrangements to pick Huang up.

小黃：

_____

_____

_____

_____

_____

_____

1. Chinese handwriting like handwriting in any other language is distinct from person to person. Look at the samples below. Can you match up each "Nǐ hǎo" with the self-identification of the person who wrote it?

你好   我姓陳

你好   我姓寇

你好.   我姓余。

你好   我姓黃

你 好   我姓向

你好!   我姓任

你好   我姓郝

你 好!   我姓田

你好,   我姓王

再見

再見

再見

再見

再见

再

見

Chinese-English Index of Reading Terms

huāyuán 花園/花园 flower garden 163, 165, 231, 233

huī 灰 grey 140

huí 回 return 61

huì 會/会 know how to, will (+ verb) 84

huíjiā 回家 return home 174–5

huì shuō 會說/会说 know how to say/speak 57, 60, 62

húntun 餛飩/馄饨 wonton, dumplings 217–8, 221

húntuntāng 餛飩湯/馄饨汤 wonton soup 217–8

huǒ 火 fire 11

huǒtuǐ 火腿 ham 204

huòzhe 或者 or 83–4, 208

hùshi 護士/护士 nurse 49, 52–3

j

jī 雞/鸡 chicken 203, 208–9

jǐ 幾/几 how many 40–1

jiā 加 plus, to add 140, 143

jiǎ 甲 "A" 52, 151

jiákè 夾克/夹克 jacket 131, 133

jiān 煎 pan fry 211, 213, 215, 224

jiàn 見/见 see, call upon (a superior) 89

jiàn 件 general measure word for clothes 131–3

jiāngcōngjī 薑蔥雞/姜葱鸡 ginger-green onion chicken 217–8

jiānglái 將來/将来 in the future 50–1, 63

jiǎo 角 ten cents, ten-cent units 109–11, 115–8

jiào 叫 be called 19–20

jiǎoluò 角落 corner 170–1

jiàoshì 教室 classroom 74, 193–7

jiāotōng 交通 traffic 247, 250

jiàowù zhǔrèn 教務主任/教务主任 dean 199–201

jiàoyuán 教員/教员 instructor 199, 201

jiǎozi 餃子/饺子 dumplings, gyoza 206, 209, 217–8, 220

jiàqián 價錢/价钱 price 118

jiārén 家人 family 63–4

jiāyóuzhàn 加油站 gas station 81, 237

jǐ diǎn zhōng 幾點鐘/几点钟 at what time 83–4

jīdīng 雞丁/鸡丁 diced chicken 213–5

jiē 街 street 40, 42

jiè 借 borrow, lend 179–80

jiějie 姐姐 elder sister 61–4

jiē rén 接人 pick up an arrival 236, 239

jiéshù 結束/结束 end, conclude 186, 190

jī lèi 雞類/鸡类 chicken category 219, 221

jīn 斤 pound 45, 47

jīn 金 gold 142–3

jǐngchá 警察 police officer 49–50

jīngguò 經過/经过 pass by 248, 250

jīngjìrén 經紀人/经纪人 realtor 163, 165

jīnglǐ 經理/经理 manager 50–1, 53

jǐ niánjí 幾年級/几年级 which grade 40, 43

jìniànpǐn 紀念品/纪念品 souvenir 231

jìniàntáng 紀念堂/纪念堂 Memorial Hall 249–50

jìnlai 進來/进来 come in 153, 158, 160

jīnnián 今年 this year 106

jìnrù 進入/进入 enter 245, 250

jīntiān 今天 today 83, 99–101

jìnzhǐ 禁止 prohibited 154, 160, 245, 250

jírì 即日 today (literary) 61, 212

jiǔ 九 nine 9–10

jiǔ 玖 nine (capital form) 113

jiǔ diǎn bàn 九點半/九点半 half past nine 84

Jiǔlóng-Guǎngzhōu 九龍廣州/九龙广州 Kowloon-Canton 260, 262

jiù shì 就是 that's right 232–3

jiǔ shí sānshí fēn 九時三十分/九时三十分 nine thirty 84

jǐ-yuè-jǐ-rì 幾月幾日/几月几日 what date 47

jùchǎng 劇場/剧场 theater, playhouse 235, 239

juéde 覺得/觉得 think, feel 33, 89

júhóng 橘紅/橘红 orange 139–40, 143

jùyuàn 劇院/剧院 theater, playhouse 235

k

kāfēi 咖啡 coffee 142, 223–4, 226–9

kāfēisè 咖啡色 brown 140, 143

kāichē 開車/开车 to drive 259, 262

kāi qìchē 開汽車/开汽车 drive a car 237, 239

kāishǐ 開始/开始 begin, start 186, 190

kàn diànshì 看電視/看电视 watch T.V. 76–8, 82, 146–8

kàn diànyǐng 看電影/看电影 watch a movie 147–8

kàn péngyou 看朋友 visit a friend 82

kànshū 看書/看书 read 77–8, 82, 146–8

kǎoshì 考試/考试 exam, take an exam 186, 190

kǎshì gōngyòng diànhuà 卡式公用電話/卡式公用电话 card-operated phone 145, 148

kě 渴 thirsty 70

kè 刻 quarter hour 83

kèběn 課本/课本 textbook 177–80

kělè 可樂/可乐 cola 226–9

Kěndéjī 肯德基 Kentucky 212

kěshì 可是 but, however 63, 147–8, 208

kètīng 客廳/客厅 living room 163–5

kēxué 科學/科学 science 183–5, 188–90

kěyǐ 可以 can, may, be acceptable 188–9, 214–5

kǒu 口 mouth 11

kuàicān 快餐 fast food 223, 228

kuài yìdiǎn 快一點/快一点 hurry up 158, 160

kùzi 褲子/裤子 trousers, pants 133

l

lā 拉 pull 204, 207, 209

lái diànhuà 來電話/来电话 incoming phone call, receive a call 84

láihuípiào 來回票/来回票 round-trip ticket 260, 262

lái le 來了/来了 coming 158, 160

lái xìn 來信/来信 incoming letter, receive a letter 63

lālāduì 啦啦隊 cheering squad 196

lājī dài 垃圾袋 garbage bag 127, 129

lán 藍/蓝 blue 139–43

Lǎo X 老 X Old X 23, 27

lǎoshī 老師/老师 teacher 49, 52–3

lǎoshì 老是 always, all the time 242–3, 258

lǎotóur 老頭兒/老头儿 old fellow, old man 132–3

lèi 累 tired 69

lěng 冷 cold 69

lèsè dài 垃圾袋 garbage bag 127, 129

Lǐ 李 Li, Lee (surname) 19–21, 61

liángxié 涼鞋 sandals 131

liányīqún 連衣裙/连衣裙 dress 132–3

lǐbài 禮拜/礼拜 week 96–7

lìjià 例假 holiday 95

lìshǐ 歷史/历史 history 183–5, 187, 189–90

qián 前 *in front* 153, 160

qiǎn 淺/浅 *shallow* 135–7

qiántiān 前天 *day before yesterday* 99–101

qiányuàn 前院 *front yard* 164–5

qǐchuáng 起床 *get up (from bed)* 174–5

qǐlái 起來/起来 *get up* 83–4

Qīn'àide X 親愛的/亲爱的 X *Dear X* 17, 63–4

qīng 輕/轻 *light* 135–7

qǐng 請/请 *Please.., go ahead* 15, 17

qīngcài 青菜 *vegetables* 208–9

qǐngwèn 請問/请问 *May I ask* 52–3, 83

qǐng wù tíngchē 請勿停車/请勿停车 *please don't park (here)* 16

qǐng wù xīyān 請勿吸煙/请勿吸烟 *please don't smoke* 16

qīngzhēngyú 清蒸魚/清蒸鱼 *steamed fish* 217–9

qīnqi 親戚/亲戚 *relative, kin* 200

qìqiú 氣球/气球 *balloon* 141, 143

qìshuǐ 汽水 *soda, pop* 71

qiūtiān 秋天 *autumn* 103, 105–6

qí zìxíngchē 騎自行車/骑自行车 *ride a bicycle* 259, 262

qū 區/区 *district* 37

qǔ 取 *pick up, retrieve* 93, 97

qù 去 *go* 96–7

quánpiào 全票 *full-price ticket* 235

quányú 全魚/全鱼 *whole fish* 213–5

qùnián 去年 *last year* 106

qúnzi 裙子 *skirt* 131

r

ràng 讓/让 *yield* 245, 250

rè 熱/热 *hot* 74

règǒu 熱狗/热狗 *hot dog* 207, 209

rén 人 *person* 11

rénshān-rénhǎi 人山人海 *very crowded* 232–3

rè sǐ 熱死/热死 *murderously hot* 71

rì 日 *sun, day* 11, 45

rìbào 日報/日报 *Daily News* 254, 256

Rìběn 日本 *Japan* 56–8

rìqī 日期 *date* 46

Rìyǔ 日語/日语 *Japanese* 58

róngyì 容易 *easy* 188, 190

ròupiàn 肉片 *meat slices* 215

ròusī 肉絲/肉丝 *meat slivers* 211, 213, 215

ròusīshíjǐncài 肉絲什錦菜/肉丝什锦菜 *mixed vegetables with pork* 217–8

rù 入 *enter* 160

rùkǒu 入口 *entrance* 160, 246, 250

ruò 弱 *weak* 139, 143

ruò 若 *if* 195

s

sān 三 *three* 9–10

sān 參 *three (capital form)* 113

sànbù 散步 *stroll, walk* 82, 89

Sānfānshì 三藩市 *San Francisco* 253, 255–6

sānjiǎoxíng 三角形 *triangle* 121–2, 124

sānmíngzhì 三明治 *sandwich* 204, 207, 209

sān tiān yǐhòu 三天以後/三天以后 *three days from now* 101

sēnlín 森林 *forest* 231–3

shālā 沙拉 *salad* 203, 207, 209

shān 山 *mountain* 11, 231–3

shàng cèsuǒ 上廁所/上厕所 *use the toilet* 75, 78

shāngdiàn 商店 *store, shop* 231, 239

shàng gè xīngqī 上個星期/上个星期 *last week* 99, 101

shàngwǔ 上午 *a.m.* 88, 90, 93

shātān 沙灘/沙滩 *beach* 231–3

shéi 誰/谁 *who* 19–20

shēn 深 *deep* 135–7

shēn'gāo 身高 *height* 46–7

shēngnián 生年 *year of birth* 19

shēngrì 生日 *birthday* 45, 47

shénme 甚麼/什么 *what* 19–20, 49

shí 十 *ten* 9–10

shí 什 *ten (capital form)* 112–3

shí 時/时 *hour (literary)* 81, 94

shì 是 *to be* 20

shì 市 *city* 37, 42

shì 室 *room* 40

shìchǎng 市場/市场 *market* 231, 233, 239

shíjiān 時間/时间 *time* 224

shìjiè 世界 *world* 177, 180, 183–4

shíjǐnmiàn 什錦麵/什锦面 *noodles with mixed ingredients* 217–8

shōu 收 *receive* 24–5, 27, 38–9, 93

shǒu 手 *hand* 29

shōufèi 收費/收费 *fee collected* 115

shōufèi cèsuǒ 收費廁所/收费厕所 *pay toilet* 115, 118

shòupiàochù 售票處/售票处 *ticket counter/window* 235, 239

shuāng 雙/双 *a pair* 131, 133

shuāyá 刷牙 *brush the teeth* 173–5

shūbāo 書包/书包 *bookbag* 178, 180

shūdiàn 書店/书店 *bookstore* 233, 238–9

shūfáng 書房/书房 *study* 163, 165

shuǐ 水 *water* 11

shuǐguǒ 水果 *fruit* 208–9, 224, 227–8

shuìjiào 睡覺/睡觉 *sleep* 76–8, 82

shuìzháo 睡著 *fall asleep* 89

shǔjià 暑假 *summer vacation* 186, 188–90, 255

shuōhuà 說話/说话 *speak* 84

shǔtiáo 薯條/薯条 *french fries* 212, 223, 228

shùxué 數學/数学 *mathematics* 183, 185, 189–90

shūzhuō 書桌/书桌 *desk* 169, 171

sì 四 *four* 9–10

sì 肆 *four (capital form)* 113–4

sìfāngxíng 四方形 *square* 121, 123–4

sìjì 四季 *the four seasons* 103, 105–6

sì miàn qiáng 四面牆/四面墙 *four walls* 170–1

sì tiān yǐqián 四天以前 *four days ago* 101

sòng yīyuàn 送醫院/送医院 *send to the hospital* 236, 239

suān là 酸辣 *hot and sour* 217–21

suàn le 算了 *forget it, never mind* 221

suì 歲/岁 *years (of age)* 40–2, 47, 62

t

tā 他 *s/he, him, her* 19

tā 她 *she, her* 19, 49

tài bǎo le 太飽了/太饱了 *too full* 72

Táiběi 臺北/台北 *Taipei* 253, 256

tài è 太餓/太饿 *too hungry* 72

tài lěng 太冷 *too cold* 72

tài máng 太忙 *too busy* 70, 72

tài rè 太熱/太热 *too hot* 72

Tàitai 太太 *Mrs.* 22, 24, 27; *wife*

Táiwān 臺灣/台湾 *Taiwan* 57–8

tàiyáng 太陽/太阳 *sun* 140, 143

tāmen 他們/他们 *they* 20–1

tāng 湯/汤 *soup* 203, 209

English-Chinese Index of Reading Terms

f

fair *bái* 白　34–5, 139–40, 143

fall asleep *shuì zháo* 睡着　89

family *jiārén* 家人　63–4

far from here *lí zhèr yuǎn* 離這兒遠/离这儿远　238–9

fast food *kuàicān* 快餐　223, 228

father *fùqin* 父親/父亲　63–4

February *èryuè* 二月　97

feel *juéde* 覺得/觉得　33, 89

female *nǚ* 女　24, 29, 46–7

fine *xì* 細/细　135–7

fire *huǒ* 火　11

first name *míng* 名　19, 21

fish *yú* 魚/鱼　29, 203, 208–9

fish slices *yú piàn* 魚片/鱼片　213–5

fitting, suitable *héshì* 合適/合适　131, 133

five *wǔ* 五　9–10; *伍* 111–4

floor *dìbǎn* 地板　169, 171

flower garden *huāyuán* 花園/花园　163, 165, 231, 233

fly, take a plane *zuò fēijī* 坐飛機/坐飞机　259, 262

foot *chǐ* 尺　45

foreign language *wàiyǔ* 外語/外语　183, 187, 190

forest *sēnlín* 森林　231–3

Forget it. Never mind. *Suàn le.* 算了　221

forget to bring *wàng le dài* 忘了帶/忘了带　178, 180

four *sì* 四　9–10; 肆　113–4

four days ago *sì tiān yǐqián* 四天以前　101

four seasons *sìjì* 四季　103, 105–6

four walls *sì miàn qiáng* 四面牆/四面墙　170–1

France *Fǎguó* 法國/法国　56, 58

freeway, highway *gāosù gōnglù* 高速公路　246, 250

french fries *shǔtiáo* 薯條/薯条　212, 223, 228

French-style *Fǎ shì* 法式　203

fried chicken *zhá jī* 炸雞/炸鸡　212–3, 215, 217–8

fried rice *chǎofàn* 炒飯/炒饭　204, 209

friend *péngyǒu* 朋友　63, 199–201

from (a place or time) *yóu* 由　55, 260, 262

front yard *qián yuàn* 前院　164–5

fruit *shuǐguǒ* 水果　208–9, 224, 227–8

fruit juice *guǒ zhī* 果汁　224, 226–9

full *bǎo* 飽/饱　70

full-price ticket *quán piào* 全票　235

fun; cute *hǎowán* 好玩　242–3

g

garbage bag *lèsè dài/lājī dài* 垃圾袋　127, 129

gas station *jiāyóuzhàn* 加油站　81, 237

gate *mén* 門/门　29

geography *dìlǐ* 地理　183, 185, 189–90

Germany *Déguó* 德國/德国　56–8

get up *qǐlái* 起來/起来　83–4

get up, rise *qǐchuáng* 起床　174–5

ginger-green onion chicken *jiāngcōngjī* 薑蔥雞/姜葱鸡　217–8

girl *nǚháir* 女孩兒/女孩儿　62, 64; *nǚháizi* 女孩子　62, 64

girls' dormitory *nǚshēng sùshè* 女生宿舍　193–4, 197

give *gěi* 給/给　127, 129

go *qù* 去　96–7

go out *chūqu* 出去　153

go shopping *mǎi dōngxi* 買東西/买东西　82

go straight ahead *zhí zǒu* 直走　248, 250

go this way *yóu cǐ qù* 由此去　55

gold *jīn* 金　142–3

good enough *gòuhǎo* 夠好/够好　137

good for the health *duì shēntǐ hǎo* 對身體好/对身体好　208, 213, 215

goodbye *zàijiàn* 再見/再见　15, 17

good-looking *hǎokàn* 好看　33–5

grade level *niánjí* 年級/年级　41

graduate *bìyè* 畢業/毕业　184, 190

graduate student *yánjiūshēng/yánjiùshēng* 研究生　44

grand avenue *dàjiē* 大街　38

green *lǜ* 綠/绿　139–43

grey *huī* 灰　140

grow up *zhǎng dà* 長大/长大　49, 53

Guilin *Guìlín* 桂林　253, 255–6

gymnasium *tǐyùguǎn* 體育館/体育馆　193, 197

gyoza, dumplings *jiǎozi* 餃子/饺子　206, 209, 217–8, 220

h

half past nine *jiǔ diǎn bàn* 九點半/九点半　84

ham *huǒtuǐ* 火腿　204

hamburger *hànbǎo* 漢堡/汉堡　223, 228

hand *shǒu* 手　29

hard to say *nánshuō* 難説/难说　256

hat *màozi* 帽子　141, 143

hate *tǎoyàn* 討厭/讨厌　141, 143

have a holiday, be on vacation *fàngjià* 放假　186, 190

have eaten already *chī guò le* 吃過了/吃过了　78

have free time *yǒu kòng* 有空　100–1

Hawaii *Xiàwēiyí* 夏威夷　63

heart, mind *xīn* 心　29

heavy *zhòng* 重　45

heavy cloud cover *duō yún* 多雲/多云　254, 256

height *shēn'gāo* 身高　46–7

hello *nǐ hǎo* 你好　16–7

high school *gāozhōng* 高中　44

Hindi *Yìndùhuà* 印度話/印度话　58

history *lìshǐ* 歷史/历史　183–5, 187, 189–90

holiday *lìjià* 例假　95

Hong Kong *Xiānggǎng* 香港　57–8, 112–3, 253, 256

hope *xīwàng* 希望　232–3

horse *mǎ* 馬/马　29

hospital *yīyuàn* 醫院/医院　233, 236, 239

hot *rè* 熱/热　74

hot and sour *suān là* 酸辣　217–21

hot dog *règǒu* 熱狗/热狗　207, 209

hotel *lǚguǎn* 旅館/旅馆　231–2, 237–9

hour (literary) *shí* 時/时　81, 94

How are you doing? *Nǐ zěnmèyàng?* 你怎麼樣/你怎么样　69, 72

however, but *kěshì* 可是　63, 147–8, 208

how many *jǐ* 幾/几　40–1

how much money *duōshǎoqián* 多少錢/多少钱　117–8

how tall *duó gāo* 多高　47

hundred *bǎi* 百　45–6, 109, 116–8; 佰　112, 114

hungry *è* 餓/饿　69–71

Index of Characters Taught for Writing